WHY PROPERTY VALUES RISE

Terry Ryder

WHY PROPERTY VALUES RISE

Understanding where to buy outperforming real estate

MAJOR
STREET

MAJOR STREET

First published in 2025 by Major Street Publishing Pty Ltd
info@majorstreet.com.au | majorstreet.com.au

NATIONAL LIBRARY OF AUSTRALIA — A catalogue record for this book is available from the National Library of Australia

Printed book ISBN: 978-1-923186-37-8
Ebook ISBN: 978-1-923186-38-5

Cover design by Tess McCabe
Internal design by Production Works

10 9 8 7 6 5 4 3 2 1

Disclaimer

The material in this publication is in the nature of general comment only, and neither purports nor intends to be advice. Readers should not act on the basis of any matter in this publication without considering (and if appropriate taking) professional advice with due regard to their own particular circumstances. The author and publisher expressly disclaim all and any liability to any person, whether a purchaser of this publication or not, in respect of anything and the consequences of anything done or omitted to be done by any such person in reliance, whether whole or partial, upon the whole or any part of the contents of this publication.

Contents

Contents

Introduction

Introduction

Imagine you know what you're doing. You know why property values rise, and you've got a plan.

Here's the story so far. In 2020 you ignored all the negative media about COVID-19 causing prices to collapse and the widely held view that Adelaide was a no-growth economy with a low-growth property market. You bought a three-bedroom, two-bathroom house on an 800-square-metre corner block in one of the city's northern suburbs for $310,000 – about the median price for the area. Rents were strong, and the gross rental yield was above 6%. Investors in Melbourne and Sydney, where 3% is generous, would be envious.

Fast forward to 2025, and similar houses are selling for $650,000 to $700,000 – more than double five years ago. Rents have risen too. Vacancies are below 1% in most Adelaide postcodes. You're now getting $550 per week; your rental return, based on your purchase price, is above 9%.

That's fortunate, because interest rates actually dropped multiple times in your first two years of ownership. However, they rose 13 times up to November 2023, massively changing the cashflow equation. Your property has positive cashflow and has already earned you over $300,000 in capital growth.

Clearly, you're a genius – you knew something that most people did not.

In reality, this is property investment 101. You buy at an affordable price in a location that has the credentials for out-performance, and you get excellent capital growth *and* a high rental return. Many Australians – newspaper readers, specifically – think you can have one or the other but not both. They're wrong.

This investment has another priceless quality: the potential to add value. Because of the land size and the council zoning, this property can be subdivided. You could create a second dwelling, and the land would effectively be free. You might spend $500,000 building a new three- or four-bedroom home, and it could be worth over $700,000 on completion. Add the $310,000 spent buying the original property and you've spent a total of $810,000 on two properties with a market value of perhaps $1.4 million in one of the most compelling growth cities in Australia.

There will have been other costs along the way, of course, but you've made serious gains in five years. And that means you have equity, and you can think about buying more investment properties and repeating the experience you had in Adelaide.

In 10 years, you probably won't need a day job.

But you're not a genius. You're simply doing real estate investment the way it's meant to be done. Simple, basic, sensible investing based on understanding why property values rise.

You went about it the right way. You wrote down your goals. You sought advice from experts on a strategy to achieve your objectives. You spoke to an accountant who understands real estate. You consulted a lawyer about structures and contracts before looking for something to buy. You had a session with a mortgage broker to determine your borrowing capacity. You got pre-approval. You spent some money on research, which told you that, contrary to popular belief in 2020, Adelaide was set to become a compelling outperformer because significant change was happening. (Five years of strong growth followed.)

Then, you started looking for a smart investment in a location with growth potential, in a city on the rise, underpinned by a vibrant economy.

You're not a genius, but you are special. Exceptional, in fact. Because most Australians don't go about it that way. And as a result, most Australians don't achieve the positive outcomes of the Adelaide scenario.

That's why everyone who wants to succeed in real estate investment needs to read this book. If you understand why property values rise – and, in particular, why they escalate in some places more than in others – then you have the keys to the kingdom of real estate success.

Location is king

The premise of this book is that *where* you buy is more important than *what* you buy or *when*. There are other members of the investment royal family, but location is king. Fundamentally, real estate is very local in nature; understand that and you have a shot at making progress.

Ideally, you will make the perfect investment decision every time. You will buy the right property at the right time in the best of all locations. Ah, if only it were that simple. Few people are that smart – or lucky.

If you can get one thing right, nail the "location" part of the equation. It may not be the best house in the best street, and you may have bought after prices had already started to rise, but if it's in a great location, you should do well – over time.

In this book you will learn what's important about location. It's not the street, nor the suburb, but the broader location that matters – the town, city or local government area (LGA). You will learn the key elements of proximity, what it's important to be near – and it's not the CBD, or the beach, or the "prime" suburbs in the biggest cities.

Real estate abounds with myths and misconceptions. This book busts them and replaces them with a research-based set of key criteria. You will read news you can use.

How can prices keep on rising and rising?

Simon Pressley of Propertyology is the nation's number one real estate tragic. He has studied Australia's housing market like no one else I know. He has gone to libraries and archives to read newspapers back through the decades to the early part of the 20th century, and he has confirmed my own observation: the plaintive modern cry that young Australians are locked out of the market and doomed to a lifetime of renting is an echo of similar statements made 20 years ago, and in the 1980s, and in the 1960s. Indeed, Pressley says, "There are front page news stories as far back as 1904 saying Australia has a housing crisis, we're not building enough, it's too expensive and tenants will never be able to afford to buy a home. We were saying that 121 years ago and we've said it every year since".

Yes, the national debate about housing affordability, the inexorable rise of prices and the growing separation between incomes and housing values has been playing out daily in news media for over a century. Yet, prices continue to rise. According to the Australian Bureau of Statistics (ABS), median house prices in 1980 were $68,850 in Sydney, $39,500 in Melbourne and $35,475 in Brisbane; in mid-2025, according to PropTrack (which is part of realestate.com.au), they were $1.471 million in Sydney, $902,000 in Melbourne and $998,000 in Brisbane.

We've been told for years that housing in Australia is simply unaffordable. Some reports claim that Sydney is the least affordable city in the world. Those reports fail to back their claims with credible evidence. The contention that no one can afford to buy is implausible; if that were true, nothing would be selling and prices would be in freefall. Yet, despite many saying it's unsustainable, the price-to-income ratio keeps rising.

In 2005, AMP Capital's chief economist Shane Oliver announced to a breathless media that there could be no price growth anywhere in Australia for the next 10 years. He had a formula that declared where Australian house prices *should* be, and values had strayed beyond the decreed band of what was reasonable. He said, "House prices are at least 25% over-valued and may not start to rise again for another decade". The *ABC* reported at the time that, according to Oliver, prices nationally "would slide a further 10% over 2005".

It made sense to many economists, journalists and others at the time, but history shows that Oliver was spectacularly wrong. Sydney's median house price rose from $520,000 in 2005 to $730,000 in 2015, according to the Australian Bureau of Statistics (ABS), having grown 19% in FY2015 alone. Melbourne's median house price rose from $330,000 to $720,000 over that same 10-year period.

The past 20 years are littered with the fractured egos of economists and others who have declared that Australian house prices are too high and must fall. There's a long history of forecasters, presented as credible experts and given considerable media exposure, warning of the impending collapse of our property values. And they've all been wrong. Economists keep saying it can't be so, but buyers keep competing for homes and prices keep rising. The market is agnostic to economic theories and the indignation of commentators like Shane Oliver and ABC talking head Alan Kohler who rage against the rise and rise of property values. It responds to the fundamentals that dictate outcomes.

Australia is a prosperous nation and there is considerable wealth here. Finance is readily available. The culture of home ownership is strong. The pursuit of wealth through real estate, by all kinds of buyers, is a powerful force. In times of economic disruption, such as the COVID period, real estate thrives, because Australians trust the solidity of bricks and mortar.

Despite media claims that no one can afford to buy, first-home-buyer activity is high. Two-income families can get loans. People willing to make compromises and sacrifices can get a foot on the property ladder. If it's their first home, there are all kinds of government assistance to get them over the line. Wealthy Baby Boomers give their adult kids a leg up, with close to 20% of first-home buyers using a handout from their parents. Those who can't afford a house can get started with a townhouse or apartment. If they still can't afford a home in an expensive city, they can become rentvestors (who invest in property while renting their home) or stayvestors (who invest in property while living with their parents) and invest in property in regional areas to eventually buy their own home.

Governments have a vested interest in high property values, which allow them to earn over $100 billion a year in real estate taxes even though owner-occupiers, who comprise three-quarters of property buyers, pay no capital gains tax. Politicians claim they care about affordability and promise to fix it, but they never deliver. Their policies have made the creation of new dwellings incredibly expensive – including the massive taxation component and the bureaucracy that has made the housing industry half as productive as the 1990s, according to the Productivity Commission – and that high cost underpins the rising values of existing homes.

They fuel demand through handouts and schemes to aid buyers, putting further upward pressure on prices, but never promote policies that deal with the high cost of dwellings or the shortage of rental homes.

An enormously powerful combination of desire, culture and competition drives property values ever higher – especially now with the rusted-on shortage. We simply can't produce enough new homes to keep up with demand fuelled by high population growth thanks to high levels of new residents from overseas. ABS data shows that household wealth in Australia hit $17 trillion in the March 2025 quarter, and almost two-thirds of that was the real estate we own.

Buying real estate is not like buying vegetables. Outside of pandemics or weather disasters, there's no shortage of potatoes for anyone entering a supermarket, and you don't have to outbid other shoppers to secure the evening meal. In real estate, however, all it takes for the price of a home to rise is for two parties to want it and be willing to pay more to win.

The bottom line is this: no one can claim that property values are too high when the average cost of creating a new house-and-land package in our cities is almost $1 million.

Let's be clear – prices sometimes fall

I don't claim that property prices always rise. I doubt anyone is silly enough to make that claim. Recent history is full of periods of prices falling, including the post-boom corrections in Sydney and Melbourne in 2018 and 2019; the prolonged downturns in Perth and Darwin after 2013, when the resources investment boom ended; and the (brief) decline that occurred in some locations after the 2020 and 2021 COVID boom.

Over time, however, property prices do rise in most locations of substance. My purpose is to explain why they do and why some locations experience greater uplift than others.

In the 20 years to 2024, house prices tripled in Adelaide and regional Tasmania, but Darwin rose a relatively muted 136%. How come?

The median price for apartments in one of the nation's most iconic locations, Surfers Paradise, was lower in 2020 than a decade earlier, but over the next five years, prices exploded. What changed?

Before the recent Perth boom that transformed it into a national leader on value growth, its property market endured a decade of weak prices, just like the Sunshine Coast. Why that poor performance? And why the dramatic change that followed?

Read on to find out.

ACT ONE
THE PROBLEM

Millions of Australians aspire to own a portfolio of properties. It embodies financial independence for them, and they believe that it will allow them to retire early.

However, few achieve the dream. The official data shows that most Australians who invest own just one property. A few more own two. These two groups comprise 90% of investment property owners. Those who own more than five investment properties comprise less than 1% of the total.

Why do so few achieve this commonly shared objective? The answer is that most do it badly.

Most Australians have limited comprehension of why property prices do what they do. There's a vague belief in the concept of capital growth but no depth of understanding. Everyone in real estate wants capital growth, but very few have any idea why it happens or where to look for it. Simon Pressley of Propertyology says, "The truth is most people ... that includes federal and state governments, city councils, economists, banks, property developers, real estate agents, buyers' agents, mortgage brokers – [are] all absolutely clueless about the very complicated dynamics of property markets".

My conversations with consumers over many years have left a strong impression that most people have their heads full of myths and misconceptions. Real estate is not taught in schools, and there's little in mainstream media that bridges the education gap. Indeed, it's awash with misinformation.

The problem for consumers seeking guidance about real estate is this: they absorb the words of journalists who know little about real estate and quote economists who know even less. To have the best chance of success, it's important first to understand the pitfalls – and how you can avoid falling prey to them.

Chapter 1

Forecasts aren't facts

The coverage of housing markets today is the worst I have seen in over four decades of researching and writing about the subject. Misinformation outweighs quality analysis, to the detriment of real estate consumers. In fact, it may seem a sweeping and exaggerated statement, but I believe most articles on housing markets are misinformation.

Real journalism does not happen in the real estate space. Few who write articles about real estate have any expertise in the industry. Most are young, inexperienced journalists rewriting press releases or simply publishing them verbatim. This means someone's propaganda is being presented to the public as news. The generators of that content have a vested interest in the message and the free publicity, which provides an incentive for sensationalism.

In the rare instances when reporters seek an alternative view to the press-release content, far too often they phone an economist. This exacerbates the misinformation. Asking an economist for an analysis of residential real estate is as smart as hiring a hockey expert to provide commentary on the AFL Grand Final. Few of the most high-profile economists – those in senior positions with the major banks and other big institutions – are specialists in residential real estate, and they regularly get it wrong, often spectacularly so. If you think I'm being unkind, compare the forecasts of big-bank economists at the start of any of the past five years with the eventual outcomes, and see if you can find one whose forecasts were right.

The media goes crazy over wacko forecasts

In 2016, I researched media predictions about real estate and compared the forecasts with the subsequent outcomes. My results highlighted the poor track record of spruikers, economists and other attention-seekers in forecasting outcomes in our housing markets – and the nonchalance with which the media publishes the most nonsensical forecasts.

Over the previous 15 years or so, it had become trendy to make doomsday forecasts about real estate. A popular number was 40% – that is, the standard scary prediction was a 40% drop in our property values, usually tipped to take place over the next 12 months. A celebrated example of this was when economist Steve Keen became a media darling with his forecasts, around the time of the GFC, that house values would crash 40%. Each one of those forecasts was proven wrong – unsurprisingly, because most of them had been fanciful in the extreme, and I suspect many of the forecasters themselves did not believe what they were saying. The goal was to achieve publicity; in that regard, they were successful.

Out of this research exercise I compiled a list entitled "Top 20 worst predictions about Australian property markets". Number one on this list was a US spruiker called Jordan Wirsz (don't feel bad if you've never heard of him), who visited Australia in 2012 and forecast a 60% fall in home values in a "bloodbath" to take place in the next year. He also tipped that land values would decline 90%. Can you imagine that? He was claiming that our residential land would be virtually worthless. Nothing like that has ever occurred anywhere on planet Earth, and it's difficult to comprehend why anyone would think it could happen in Australia. The most startling thing was that the Australian media gave these predictions credibility and gave the touring spruiker exactly what he wanted – loads of free publicity.

What followed this prediction was five years of major price increases in our two biggest cities and mostly steady markets in the rest of Australia. Perth and Darwin experienced moderate decline, but nowhere did values fall 60% and there was no collapse in land prices. There was no apology from the many journalists who had caused considerable alarm to families by telling them the value of their homes was likely to collapse.

Another US pontificator, Harry S. Dent, visited Australia several times in the preceding decade, and each time – including in 2011 and 2014 – warned that our property prices would crash in the next 12 months. Each time, the Australian media honoured him as a credible commentator and gave him lots of free coverage, notwithstanding his growing track record of getting his forecasts about our real estate markets utterly wrong.

My list also included local economists who had made similar predictions within specific time frames and enjoyed the same success rate. Some had claimed that according to their economic models, our homes were overvalued, and therefore prices must fall. Others stated during times of rising interest rates that the higher cost of money would cause a collapse of property values. The head of one of our major banks said in 2011 that the sovereign debt crisis in Europe would force down our property values, only to be embarrassed by several years of strong price rises. As I mentioned in my introduction to this book, high-profile and much-quoted Australian economist Shane Oliver of AMP Capital declared in 2005 that there would be no growth – none – in our home values for the next 10 years. Ouch.

Also on the list were commentators who, in 2013 and 2014, rushed to be the first to declare the end of the price boom in Sydney and Melbourne. One of them was a senior official at the Reserve Bank of Australia (RBA), while another was a Morgan Stanley analyst who famously said in June 2014 (about three years too early), "If you're an investor, you've missed the boat".

In September 2018 we had the notorious *60 Minutes* debacle, with yet another forecast of property values falling 40% based on nothing but a preconceived headline to boost ratings. At the time, virtually every independent commentator who reacted to the program said the forecast scenario was highly unlikely or plain silly. The key analysts featured on the program claimed their views were misrepresented through selective editing. I spoke to one of them, Louis Christopher of SQM Research, and he was horrified at the outcome.

In fact, I had also been approached by *60 Minutes* to take part in the program, but they had dropped the planned interview when I told them I disagreed with their basic premise of collapsing property markets. This is not how journalism is meant to work. In true journalism, you do your research and conduct your interviews, and then you come to some conclusions and decide on your headline. *60 Minutes* did it backwards by determining the headline and then seeking comment that supported it, and excluding from coverage anyone unwilling to give them the preordained soundbites. I complained to the ABC television program *Media Watch*, and they did a segment pointing out the many flaws in the *60 Minutes* segment.

Several years after that *60 Minutes* segment was broadcast, the forecast collapse had not happened – not even in the midst of a global pandemic. Indeed, prices rose in most major Australian markets in 2020, and by the March quarter of 2021 it was clear there was a nationwide property boom, with prices rising almost everywhere.

The forecasts from the big banks are frequently wrong

A future edition of the "Top 20 worst predictions" list will feature some of the bank forecasts of March and April 2020. The arrival of COVID-19 in Australia and the resulting lockdowns led to assumptions of dire economic outcomes and property values declining 15%, 20% or, in an extreme prediction from Gareth Aird of Commonwealth Bank, over 30%. Martin North of Digital Finance Analytics gave this doomsday warning: "There is a 60% chance of Australian house prices falling by 30% to 40% in 2020 due to high unemployment". Keep in mind that Australia has never had a year in which real estate values have dropped 30% across the board, or even 20%. What they were telling us to expect was unprecedented.

The price forecasts of the bank economists were all proven to be incorrect. Housing values overall rose in 2020, and by the end of that year Australia was showing strong signs of a nationwide property boom. Data from both Domain and CoreLogic confirmed that Australian house prices nationally rose 6%, with several capital cities and regional markets increasing by between 9% and 12%, and would go on to record growth of 25% in 2021. In April 2021, *Media Watch* did a segment on those dire predictions and just how wrong the big-name economists had been.

Analysts who correctly predicted these outcomes, in stark contrast to the big banks, included Stephen Koukoulas of Market Economics, James Symond of Aussie, Simon Pressley of Propertyology and myself.

By August and September 2020, the banks were all admitting that they got it wrong and were issuing new, more moderate and optimistic predictions (thereby rendering their earlier forecasts redundant). Westpac, whose March 2020 forecasts suggested massive declines in prices, were publishing reports in September 2020 predicting 2021 price growth of boom-time proportions.

When interest rates started to rise from May 2022, bank economists were eager to parade their forecasting skills and, in August, the big banks went public with their house price predictions. Given the simplistic view they all appear to share that rising rates means plummeting prices, Westpac said house prices in Melbourne and Sydney would drop 18% in the next 12 months, Commonwealth Bank said prices would drop 15% and NAB would later predict that Australian house prices would fall "as much as 20%", while ANZ declared that house prices nationally would drop 8% in 2022 and a further 9% in 2023. The news media had a field day, announcing predictions of an "epic national property price crash". Nothing of the sort occurred. Nationally house prices rose 8.1% in 2023, according to CoreLogic.

ANZ also forecast that house prices in 2023 would fall 12% in Brisbane, 12% in Perth and 17% in Adelaide. Rather ironically, and to the eternal embarrassment of ANZ economists, the opposite happened – Brisbane rose 13.3%, Adelaide 8.6% and Perth 15.6%, and those three cities went on to lead the nation with boom-level price growth up to 2025.

This inaccuracy in big-bank forecasts is all too common. Let's take NAB as a case study. The bank publishes regular forecasts about residential property prices, including its *NAB Quarterly Australian Residential Property Survey* reports. I've been reading their forecasts for many years and they are never correct. And I do mean *never*. They always err on the side of pessimism and are invariably wrong.

Here's an example. One of NAB's reports published in January 2019 predicted that capital cities on average would record a 3.8% fall in house prices and a 4.3% fall in apartment prices in 2019: Sydney's house prices would drop 5.6%, Melbourne's would decline 7.0%, Brisbane would deliver zero growth and the other state capitals would deliver minimal growth. The news media gave this considerable fanfare and treated the forecasts as facts – stating, for example, that Melbourne prices *will* fall 7% by the end of the year.

Here's what actually happened. According to a NAB report early in 2020, the average house price in the capital cities actually *rose* 2.9%, and apartments rose 3.4%. Sydney's house prices rose 6.1% and Melbourne's 4.6%.

Quite a dismal failing, isn't it? But the contrasts between the NAB forecasts and the eventual reality are even more stark when you look at the figures from more credible sources.

2019 capital growth in houses prices

	National	Sydney	Melbourne
NAB prediction, early 2019	–3.8%	–5.6%	–7.0%
NAB report, early 2020	2.9%	6.1%	4.6%
Domain	5.5%	6.8%	8.7%
CoreLogic	2.1%	6.1%	4.6%
SQM Research	2.9%	4.8%	5.7%

Why does it matter? Because individuals and families make big-money decisions based on these forecasts. I know many people who were ready to buy in 2020 and cancelled their plans because they were told property values would collapse. By the time they realised the chattering economists were wrong, values were 20% higher.

Chapter 2

The data is misleading

Australian news media is startlingly inconsistent when it comes to the treatment of real estate prices. When real data is published showing what actually happened with house prices, the media will often challenge the figures if they are positive and dismiss them as irrelevant or misleading. That's journalism, right? Journalists are supposed to challenge things. But if someone makes a *negative* forecast about prices, as big-bank economists did at the start of 2023 and 2024, they will accept that without question. Worse, they will turn this speculation into a fact – it is presented not as "prices are forecast to fall" but "prices *will* fall" or "are falling".

Data from both CoreLogic and SQM Research showed that in March and April 2020, prices resisted the impacts of the COVID shutdown and even rose to some degree in most markets around the nation. Three months into the COVID shemozzle, there was still no evidence of the price collapse predicted by the usual suspects. (Six months later, not much had changed.) But this was broadly challenged by the news media as being misleading and untenable. Most headlines early in May 2020, reporting the April price figures, were extremely negative. One media outlet managed to turn all that solid price data into this headline: "Real Estate Markets Collapse".

The May 2020 forecasts from some of the big banks were also quite negative. The news media had a field day with those reports, and no one challenged them. And they needed to be challenged, because the track records of bank economists in forecasting anything, but real estate prices in particular, are notoriously poor.

And a big reason for this is that they rely on dodgy data and have a limited understanding of real estate dynamics.

Generalised data is useless

Generalisation is the curse of the Australian real estate consumer. The average punter can't access quality information about what's really going on in property because journalists and the people they quote speak in generalisations. Most media "analysis" about housing discusses "the Australian property market" – which, as this book shows emphatically, is a mythical creature bred by economists.

We're told that "Australian property prices" are rising or falling – or, to use media parlance, skyrocketing or plummeting. When CoreLogic published its price data for June 2020, the national average situation was a decrease of 0.7%. So, according to the media (and the economists feeding them soundbites), Australian property prices were falling. No, "nose-diving". A 0.7% nose-dive.

But the CoreLogic figures also indicated that in June 2020, amid all the disruption of the pandemic, house prices rose in Canberra, Hobart, Darwin, regional New South Wales, regional Tasmania and regional South Australia. And house prices had risen in all those places in the previous quarter too, as well as in Adelaide, regional Victoria and regional Northern Territory. In other words, in the most recent quarter at that time, house prices had risen (according to CoreLogic) in nine of the 15 major market jurisdictions across Australia. But because the national average was a fall of 0.7% (dragged down by the negative results in Sydney and Melbourne), economists and journalists declared that "Australian house prices" were "plummeting", "plunging" or "collapsing", depending on the individual writing the headline and where they sat on the ethical spectrum.

In annual terms, house prices were higher than a year earlier in 12 of the 15 jurisdictions: seven of the eight capital cities and five of the seven state regional markets.

This generalised data can also be a problem one level down. In June 2020, both CoreLogic and SQM agreed that Sydney house prices had been falling, but that too was a generalisation – prices were not falling everywhere in Sydney.

Sydney overall had taken a bigger hit from the pandemic than most cities. It had the highest vacancy rate overall among the capital cities, and the rate in Sydney's CBD in particular rose to 16%, before improving slightly to 14% in June, according to SQM. Did that mean, as the media coverage implied, that vacancies were high everywhere in Sydney and prices were falling right across the metro area? Absolutely not. Some areas were thriving. The Sutherland LGA, generally known as The Shire, was a rising market. It offered an exceptional lifestyle based on proximity to water and national parks, and its real estate was considerably more affordable than in the North Shore, the Eastern Suburbs or the Inner West. The pandemic shutdown had opened more people's eyes to the possibility of working from home rather than commuting to a CBD office building, and The Shire was attracting growing demand because of this gathering trend. Vacancies in most of its postcodes were below 2% and many suburbs had rising prices. This was a growth market that defied the generalised Sydney statistics.

Similar misunderstandings about Sydney real estate were generated by shallow media coverage in mid-2025. The generalised figure from CoreLogic suggested the Sydney market was anaemic, with "Sydney house prices" up just 2% in the previous 12 months. But within Greater Sydney were specific locations with annual median price growth above 10%. In the Canterbury-Bankstown LGA, 14 suburbs had annual median price growth above 10% for either their house market or their unit market. In the City of Blacktown, Marsden Park, Riverstone, Seven Hills and Tallawong were all high-volume house markets where annual price growth exceeded 10%. And there were many other examples.

The start of 2025 also saw a different misreporting of the reality of residential real estate. After declaring there was a downturn in national real estate based on one or two months of lukewarm figures, suddenly, in the wake of February 2025 data, the media declared that the downturn was over and the boom back on. A two-month downturn had been followed by a miraculous recovery: a monthly increase in the national median price of... 0.3%. As I wrote in a social media broadcast at the time, "For a long time, the biggest problem for consumers trying to make sense of market events has been commentators placing undue importance on short-term results. Real estate is a slow-moving and long-term business – and data showing one month's change in median house prices is meaningless".

Data sources can contradict one another

However, it's not just the generalisation of real estate data that's the problem. Real estate data companies like CoreLogic, PropTrack and Domain also present flawed analysis, and often contradict one another, because they employ economists – usually young and lacking experience at the industry coalface – rather than seasoned specialists in real estate market analysis.

The ABS declared that the average Australian house price surpassed $1 million in the March 2025 quarter, but both CoreLogic and PropTrack claimed it was still below $900,000. In fact, the ABS figure was the national mean price and the other sources were using median prices, and the apparent contradiction was a source of considerable confusion.

This reinforces this point that putting faith in published data on prices is one of the great perils facing real estate consumers. Anyone who bases a major decision on something they have read about pricing levels in a location and how much they are growing (or falling) may make a serious miscalculation.

It's possible to find three sources of price information for a suburb and get three different results – one suggesting prices are rising, another claiming they're stagnating and the third declaring that they're falling. In January 2018, I googled the median house price for Alice Springs in the Northern Territory and found these three outcomes:

1. According to *Your Investment Property Magazine*, quoting CoreLogic data, the median house price was $299,950, up 5.7% over the past 12 months.
2. According to Real Estate Investar, it was $469,000, unchanged from a year earlier.
3. According to homesales.com.au, it was $1,109,913, down 1.7% on a year earlier.

So, the median price was either $300,000 or $469,000 or $1.1 million, depending on which source you chose to believe, and was either down a little, unchanged or up moderately.

If this were an isolated example, there wouldn't be a problem, but finding contradictory data on pricing is common.

For the January 2018 edition of one of my regular reports, I compared price growth for apartments in the major cities, taking figures from three major sources: the ABS, CoreLogic and SQM. And there were big differences in growth rates from one source to the next:

- **Hobart** was the clear market leader at that time – all three sources had the Tasmanian capital leading on annual growth in the median price, but there were big variations in the claimed rate of growth, ranging from 9% to 18%.

- **Melbourne** ranked second with two sources, but again, there was quite a divergence in terms of the actual growth rate – the ABS had 4%, CoreLogic had double that rate (a little over 8%) and SQM's rate of 13% was three times higher than the ABS rate.

- **Brisbane** was rather mediocre, it was broadly agreed, but SQM recorded no change in prices, while ABS had prices down a little and CoreLogic had prices declining at three times the ABS rate.

- **Canberra** was hard to rate. Two sources gave growth figures that suggested a quiet market (1.8% and 2.1%), while the third depicted a strongly rising market at 10% growth.

- **Perth** prices had stopped falling, CoreLogic data suggested, but both the ABS and SQM recorded an annual decline of about 6%.

Has anything changed more recently? In May 2025 I searched for the current median house price for Blacktown in Western Sydney. Various sources provided their version of the truth, including Domain, realestate.com.au, CoreLogic, propertyvalue.com.au and housing.id.com.au. Estimates ranged from $980,000 to $1.15 million. No two sources had the same figure. All agreed that the figure had increased in the previous 12 months, but the level of growth quoted ranged from 5.4% to 10.2%. So, Blacktown was either a place of moderate or high price growth, and it was either a million-dollar suburb or not quite.

I performed the same search the suburb of Caboolture in the far north of Greater Brisbane, and five sources provided an answer, all with different figures. The median house price ranged from $700,000 to $744,000, and the level of annual growth ranged from 12.8% to 18.8%.

Similarly, the median unit price for Melbourne, according to the latest figures from Domain, PropTrack and CoreLogic, was either $550,022 (up 3.6%), $588,000 (down 1.0%) or $610,327 (down 2.6%). That's quite some variation.

So, what do we make of that? My conclusion is that it's all dodgy data to a certain degree. The discrepancies and contradictions are partly explained by different methodologies and varying definitions about various elements, such as how you classify townhouses and where city boundaries sit.

Think about it. The greater Melbourne metropolitan area has a population over 5 million and contains over 500 suburbs, and what's happening in Toorak is somewhat different to the situation in Thomastown, while Brighton shares few similarities with Dandenong. Yet, a research company will seek to distil all the sales activity in the past 12 months down to a single growth figure.

And the vagaries of real estate statistics extend way beyond prices. There was a startling contradiction in data published on capital-city vacancy rates in June 2025: SQM Research said Darwin had the lowest vacancy rate at 0.5%, while the Real Estate Institute of Australia (REIA) declared that Darwin had the *highest* vacancy rate at 2.9%.

The media treats the data as facts

Yet, despite the constant discrepancies, the media draws sweeping conclusions from these sources. This heightens the risks for consumers, who make big-money decisions based on this data.

When publicity seekers who don't give a damn present rubbish statistics to journalists who don't know any better, the outcome is misinformation. This is most commonly seen in lists of the places where property values are growing the fastest – allegedly. These lists are mostly nonsense.

The key problem is that when the sales sample is small, the median price data is often rubbish. Every time I've examined a list, published in a major newspaper, of what are purportedly the places with the highest value growth, it has comprised mostly small country towns or tiny suburbs where there have been too few sales to produce accurate figures. My rule of thumb is that any location with fewer than 30 sales in a year will produce a median price that is likely very rubbery, and I'm sure anyone with experience in real estate statistics would tell you something similar.

The *Herald Sun* published such a list of dodgy data in May 2021. The journalist interviewed me while preparing the article. She asked me to comment on the list, which claimed to be the Top 15 locations in Victoria for value growth in the past 10 years. I told her the list was highly suspect. Only three of the 15 locations were legitimate inclusions; the other 12 were all places with fewer than 30 sales in the past year.

Top of the list was Marysville, a very small town with only 13 sales in the previous 12 months. According to the list, spat out of a computer by realestate.com.au (whose staff should know better), property values had grown 15% a year, on average, for 10 years. If this was true, every investor in Australia would be trying to buy there. But it wasn't true. It was a statistical aberration caused by a small sales sample.

I explained this to the journalist. She went ahead and published the article anyway, thereby misleading thousands of *Herald Sun* readers. She quoted me in the article, but not my comments describing why the list was a farcical piece of misinformation.

Sadly, this presentation of rubbery figures occurs frequently in mainstream media.

Chapter 3

Who can you trust?

Here's the hardest thing for consumers researching real estate to figure out: who do you believe?

To truly understand real estate dynamics, you need to know who to listen to – and who to ignore. So many people are pumping out press releases, writing commentary pieces and pontificating on television and in podcasts about housing markets – and only a fraction of this heaving mass of white noise is worthy of your attention.

Fortunately, there are markers that expose the pretenders and allow you to separate them from the genuine experts. Here are seven clues to identify the pontificators you should ignore.

1. They discuss Australian real estate as a single market

In an October 2018 article published in *The Australian,* Josh Frydenberg, then the Federal Treasurer, exposed himself as a pretender. His opening paragraph stated as a fact, "Prices in our major capital cities have fallen for 12 consecutive months". In doing so, he perpetuated one of the worst pieces of misinformation prevalent at the time. In October 2018 the average result across the eight capital cities was a negative figure, according to CoreLogic, but nine of the 14 major market jurisdictions (eight capital cities and six regional areas – they excluded the tiny regional Northern Territory market, as we also do at Hotspotting) had prices higher than a year earlier. Other research sources had different figures: SQM Research, for example, recorded the national average result as a 1.7% rise in annual terms, while the ABS recorded quarterly price rises in five of the eight capitals.

So, the claim that prices had fallen everywhere for 12 months was unsupported by the research evidence. The Federal Treasurer was simply parroting misleading media headlines. We're entitled to better.

But Frydenberg was not alone in his ignorance. Indeed, when it came to extrapolating the situation in Sydney and Melbourne at that time into a national downturn, he had lots of company. As discussed in chapters 1 and 2, economists in particular are prone to misinforming Australians by discussing the nation as a single market and generalising about prices.

The greatest cause of misinformation about real estate is the concentration of major media outlets in Australia's two biggest cities. Most of what we hear and read is written or spoken in Sydney and Melbourne. This greatly frustrates the 60% of Australians who live elsewhere.

Journalists and economists based in the two big cities think that what they see around them is Australia, and they extrapolate events in Sydney and Melbourne to generate a national scenario. However, our two biggest cities are usually the exception rather than the rule – as was the case in 2024, when smaller cities and regional markets excelled while Melbourne and Sydney struggled. Conversely, when Sydney and Melbourne were rising in the five years up to 2018, the media drew upon economist rhetoric to declare a national property boom, but there was no boom in

Brisbane, Adelaide or Canberra, and prices in both Perth and Darwin were steadily in reverse. This big-city boom was followed by a downturn that was characterised as a national calamity, with daily articles despairing over the decline of "Australian property prices" – meanwhile, Hobart was having a growth spurt; Brisbane, Adelaide and Canberra were chugging along steadily; and more and more regional cities were having up-cycles. Likewise, in the post-COVID-boom environment, the media depicted a nationwide slump, influenced by mediocre performance in Melbourne and Sydney, but other markets were thriving.

The weather map on TV news bulletins provides a useful analogy for our property markets. The highs for a spring day in 2020 were 11 degrees Celsius in Hobart, 20 in Melbourne, 15 in Canberra, 20 in Sydney, 24 in Brisbane, 26 in Adelaide, 19 in Perth and 35 in Darwin. Temperatures in regional Australia ranged from 7 to 37 degrees. Imagine trying to pick one number to describe the weather in Australia that day. Real estate has similar variances. The temperature of markets varies dramatically from one city to the next.

As an aside, one of the most significant trends impacting real estate in the past decade is people vacating Sydney and Melbourne and moving to smaller cities or regional areas. I call it the "exodus to affordable lifestyle", and it's a key reason why the biggest capital growth between 2020 and 2025 occurred in regional markets. All of the top 10 locations for capital growth over those five years were regional centres, as were 18 of the top 20. I delve more deeply into this subject later in the book.

I can't say this loudly enough: there is no such entity as the "Australian property market". In fact, it's equally invalid to discuss Sydney as a single market, or Melbourne, Brisbane or Perth; an intelligent and useful analysis will recognise that there are markets within markets. The Sydney metropolitan area has over

650 suburbs in 33 municipalities. There are tens of thousands of transactions every year in markets as varied as Manly and Penrith, Bondi Beach and Campbelltown – all doing their own thing, all driven by local events – and distilling all of that into a single figure that purports to describe "Sydney property prices" is ludicrous. There's little value in telling people that Sydney house prices rose 2% to 3% in 2024 when some suburbs recorded changes well above 10% – including many in the Canterbury-Bankstown LGA, as one example – and others experienced falling property values. But that's what the research firms do in their pursuit of cheap publicity, and media is happy to facilitate their pursuit of an easy headline.

Real estate is very local in nature, and generalised commentary is misinformation. As veteran adviser, commentator and author Noel Whittaker (someone with real credentials) put it, "How can you compare a townhouse in Cairns with a mansion in Point Piper? All over Australia some markets may be rising, other markets may be falling, and some may be flat". The challenge for real estate consumers is to understand what makes some markets hot while others are mild or cold.

Next time you hear or read a commentator discussing "the Australian property market", or claiming that "Australian house prices have fallen 5%" or "unit prices are up 6.5%", turn the page or change channels, because the writer or talking head is a charlatan.

2. They're not real estate specialists

The problem with Josh Frydenberg was that, while he may have been a capable Treasurer, he is not a real estate expert. Residential property is not his thing.

This is the core problem with many of the prolific pontificators: they frequently err in thinking they can transfer their financial knowledge and economic theories to real estate. After four decades as a real estate specialist, I'm still waiting to encounter an economist who understands the dynamics of housing markets.

Most of the people who made my 2016 "Top 20 worst predictions about Australian real estate" list by getting their predictions spectacularly wrong were economists who strayed outside their area of specialty.

Alan Kohler, a high-profile commentator on business and share market matters, has recently become the pin-up lad for economists who like to lecture to property markets. Kohler has a serious bee in his bonnet about housing, its unshakeable presence in Australian culture and the way it keeps producing capital growth. He tends to blame it all on the alleged tax advantages provided to property investors, a view that is both simplistic and plain wrong. It overlooks the reality that most consumers competing for real estate are home buyers, that home buyers are the tax-advantaged entities in the market (because they pay no capital gains tax or land tax and pay lower levels of stamp duty and council rates than investors) and that those alleged tax advantages for investors play no part in the high cost of creating new dwellings, nor in the overall shortage of dwellings that puts upward pressure on prices and rents.

Shane Oliver, chief economist for AMP Capital, is another talking head much loved by lazy journalists because he can always be relied upon to say something sensationally negative about residential real estate. His track record on forecasting property price outcomes is arguably the worst in the nation.

The problem with Kohler and Oliver is that real estate is not their area of expertise. They turn their focus to it occasionally and always look at it through the prism of economic theories about what property prices *should* do – and when something different invariably happens, they admonish real estate for not behaving itself. There are many others out there like Kohler and Oliver, collectively misinforming consumers.

True real estate experts worthy of your attention are genuine specialists for whom researching markets is a daily routine. They don't treat real estate data as a vehicle for free publicity but as a means to inform the public by presenting well-considered and balanced analysis. They include people like Simon Pressley of Propertyology; Ben Kingsley of Empower Wealth, who is also a director of the Property Investors Council of Australia; Nicola McDougall of Bricks and Mortar Media, who is also a real estate author and until July 2025 was president of Property Investment Professionals of Australia (PIPA); Arjun Paliwal of InvestorKit; Melinda Jennison of Streamline Property Buyers, who is also president of the Real Estate Buyers Agents Association of Australia (REBAA); and Gavin Hegney, a valuer and investor and one of the sharpest real estate analysts in the land. They are genuine, devoted and independent experts who specialise in residential property and have earned the right to be heard by being research-driven and having experience at the ground level of real estate markets. They each know more about residential property than the Big Four banks' senior economists combined.

I don't include on my list of credible experts the high-profile data businesses like CoreLogic, Domain and PropTrack. These organisations have lots of statistics on residential real estate but an unhappy knack of employing the wrong people as their spokespeople – usually young and stylish, with heads full of economic theories, but lacking in real-world nous. They need to get out more and spend some time at the coalface speaking to people who live and breathe real estate every day.

3. They believe it's all about interest rates

Here's what passes for analysis in residential property: if event A coincides with event B, then logically, event B must have caused event A. It's a theory that ignores events C, D, E and F, all of which may have had an influence.

Most of the pretenders talk about the level of interest rates as the prime determinant of real estate markets. Ask your average economist why Sydney boomed from 2013 to 2017 (event A) and they will tell you it was because of "record low interest rates" (event B). Event B coincided with event A, and so, according to many of our chattering economists, event B caused event A. Obviously. Fast-forward to late 2020 and early 2021 and real estate is pumping strongly in many parts of Australia (event A), and we still have "record low interest rates" (event B), so again, event B must have caused event A.

This is embarrassing for several reasons. If interest rates were the catalyst, why no boom in Brisbane from 2013 to 2017, or in Adelaide, Canberra and most of regional Australia? And why did prices fall in Perth and Darwin? In fact, Melbourne was the only other strong market. Apparently, the laws of financial physics applied only to our two biggest cities. Curious.

It's false logic to assume, as many economists do, that low rates equals boom and rising rates equals downturn. It may appear to make sense, but the opposite is true. The two biggest nationwide property booms of the past 50 years (by which I mean genuine nationwide booms extending over two or three years, which are rare) – the first in the late 1980s, and the second in the early part of the 21st century – both occurred during periods of high and rising interest rates. Interest rates were high in those times because the national economy was raging and the authorities were seeking to keep a lid on things by lifting rates. At times like these, consumer sentiment is high and confidence strong – and that's when we're most likely to have a national property boom.

Why did Sydney and Melbourne boom from 2013 to 2017 when most locations across Australia did not? Because the underlying economies in those places were very much the exception. At that time, New South Wales and Victoria had by far the strongest economies in the land, led by their capital cities, where infrastructure spending totalling tens of billions of dollars generated economic activity and jobs. The Australian economy overall, though, while not weak, was struggling. The RBA dropped the official interest rate at various times to create stimulus, but consumer sentiment was lukewarm. Brisbane's market failed to replicate the Sydney and Melbourne booms, while many regional markets in Queensland (like Gladstone, Emerald, Moranbah, Dalby, Townsville and others) had falling prices. Prices in Perth and Darwin fell steadily, and some regional centres (like Port Hedland and Karratha) suffered spectacular declines in their property markets. Low interest rates did little to help them.

The end of the Sydney–Melbourne booms and the subsequent correction (in 2018 and 2019) occurred with interest rates still at those very low levels. In 2020 and 2021, economists were still seeking to explain real estate outcomes with "record low interest rates" as the prime influence, but we still had record low interest rates when that short, sharp boom stopped. Sadly, that's all they've got to offer in terms of market analysis, and it doesn't matter how often they are wrong – they will never see real estate differently.

In 2024 we had stubbornly high interest rates, after 13 increases by the RBA from May 2022 until November 2023 and then no change throughout 2024. According to the loudly proclaimed theory of bank economists, that should mean falling property prices, and the forecasts at the start of 2023 and 2024 were indeed for substantial price decline across Australia. So, did house prices fall? According to the price report published by CoreLogic in early January 2025, "Australian home values were up 4.9% in 2024, adding approximately $38,000 to the median value of a home". During the year, Perth home values rose 19.1%, Adelaide 13.1% and Brisbane 11.2%. The average result in the nation's regional markets was a rise of 6.0%. The only major market to record a significant decline was Melbourne, where the median home value dropped 3.0%. PropTrack reported similar figures.

In February 2025 the RBA delivered the first reduction in the official interest rate since November 2020. Over the following three months, every positive event in real estate anywhere in Australia – strong auction results, house prices rising in some cities in April, a month-on-month increase in new-home sales – was attributed by economists to the rate cut. They failed to explain the places where house prices fell or the auctions that failed. And then in May 2025 when the RBA announced another rate reduction, the misinformation machine went into overdrive. Economists, analysts and commentators were tripping over each other in their haste to forecast soaring property prices. We were told to expect a boom because of two small reductions after 13 increases. I call it kindergarten analysis.

The clear message in all these scenarios is that there are market forces driving price outcomes that are far more influential than interest rate levels. Simon Pressley of Propertyology says, "Interest rates have a very small impact on property market performance. In most cases, they have no impact at all".

They say that if you torture statistics enough, they'll tell you anything you want to hear. If you believe in a theory, you can cherry-pick data that appears to support your cherished belief and ignore anything that contradicts it.

The genuine expert, by contrast, will discuss individual markets, including different submarkets within each of our major cities, and will understand the fundamental importance of the underlying local economies – influenced by population trends, infrastructure spending, jobs creation and supply-demand factors – in determining real estate outcomes.

4. They measure markets with median price data and auction clearance rates

Real estate is rife with dodgy data sets, and the dodgiest of all are median price data and auction clearance rates. The media is obsessed with them; apparently, they are the barometers that matter. However, both are blunt instruments for measuring markets and are often rubbery figures.

Median price data is full of anomalies and is often misused by journalists, who interpret a 10% change in median price as a 10% change in property values. Often, it means nothing of the sort. Median price data plays a part in market analysis, and I use it daily, but it must be handled with caution and in association with other data.

Auction clearance rates are even worse. I've conducted extensive research on the difference between published clearance rates and the true ones, and so has Louis Christopher of SQM Research, one of the nation's most experienced real estate analysts. We agree that the true clearance rate is usually several percentage points below the published one. Many auction results – mostly the failed ones – are never reported and don't get included in the figures published by the media.

There are other, better ways to gauge the health of a property market. Sales volume is one; vacancy rates is another. Rental movements, days on market, listings of properties for sale... At Hotspotting, we use a combination of all those factors in assessing local property markets. A full assessment of the health and direction of an individual property market needs to include a range of data sets.

Sales volume is one of the best measures of markets. For the past decade I've analysed sales activity data every quarter, because it's a forward indicator – I've found it to be an accurate way to predict where prices are most likely to rise in the near future. Discussion of sales activity as a key metric permeates this book.

5. They say to follow population growth

Over many years tracking Australian real estate markets I have observed "experts" advising consumers that the best strategy for success is to follow the population growth. It's a simplistic approach with elements of high risk.

My observation is that population growth doesn't lead price growth, it follows it. But it's easy to be deceived.

Population data published in May 2025 showed that of the 50 largest cities and towns in Australia, the Sunshine Coast led the nation in population growth over five years, growing 12.9%. It was also one of the national leaders on price growth over five years. The alignment of those two data points might suggest that population growth creates price growth.

The truth is a little more complicated. What matters is the local economy and everything happening in it. If the local economy is strong and creating employment, perhaps boosted by major infrastructure projects, the local population will grow as people move to the area to take up those jobs, particularly if the area offers lifestyle benefits. That demand drives up prices, particularly if housing supply is low and can't keep up with the rising demand.

That was the Sunshine Coast over the past decade. When the infrastructure investment boom was at its peak, including a new $2 billion hospital complex, this region was recording unprecedented price growth. Top-end suburbs such as Sunshine Beach saw house prices double in three years. Rising population fuelled the price growth, but the key factor was the economy, which generated the jobs, which attracted the new population.

Population growth can be misleading. The highest growth often occurs in new development areas on the fringes of our major cities because there is land available for new housing estates. Think Melton in the west of the Greater Melbourne area, or the growth corridor between the Gold Coast and the Greater Brisbane area. There have been times in recent history when property values have fallen in these locations. With so much greenfield land available, developers have overshot and built too many homes. As I observe elsewhere in this book, oversupply is the one factor that can trash property values.

Amid the population data published in May 2025, a new growth area was delivering startling figures: the Morisset-Cooranbong district in the City of Lake Macquarie on the fringe of Newcastle. Morisset, once a sleepy fishing village on the edge of Australia's largest coastal saltwater lake, is a new development area where the population is projected to triple in 20 years. But Cooranbong's median house price graph largely flatlined in the three years to mid-2025. It's the availability of land that has been creating the population spike, and it's not an indicator of outperformance on value growth.

Here's another way to look at it. Many established suburban areas have little or no population growth because they're well-established and built out, with no underutilised land; only when someone demolishes houses and builds apartments, if zonings allow, can the local population rise. Yet despite the lack of population growth, they can experience significant capital growth. The middle-ring precinct in Brisbane's north is a case in point: its population growth over the past 10 years has been only fractional, but most suburbs have five-year capital growth rates of 12% or more per year, with the best house market averaging 15% and the best unit market 16% per year (meaning values double in less than five years).

The biggest impact of population growth on real estate is overseas migration on the supply-and-demand equation. In a time of unprecedented housing shortage, Australia's population has been rising sharply, largely through migration. The ABS population figures in June 2025 showed that the national population had passed 27 million, following a rise of 445,900 in 2024, and most of that (340,800) came from net overseas migration; natural increase (births minus deaths) contributed only 105,200. At the same time, the National Housing Supply and Affordability Council said Australia was on track to fall 262,000 homes short of the federal government's five-year target of 1.2 million new dwellings. The chronic housing shortage will likely get worse, exacerbated by inflated population growth.

6. They say not to invest in areas with above-average crime rates

Whenever I speak at seminars or webinars, audience feedback often portrays a lack of knowledge about what works in real estate. In deciding where to buy, people obsess over issues that simply don't matter – income levels in individual suburbs, or the level of social housing in the area, or the ratio of home owners versus investors.

One of the great furphies in real estate is that areas with above-average crime rates are bad places to invest. Many investors fixate on this. They will reject any location they perceive as being downmarket, stigmatised or having high crime. I've always thought this was wobbly thinking and a case of real estate snobs trying to justify an attitude.

According to an October 2020 report from Pete Wargent, co-founder of BuyersBuyers.com.au, housing in high-crime areas across Sydney and Melbourne has outperformed the property market over time: "Despite the stigma ... and the potential challenges that go with that over the short term, over a reasonable time frame this has tended to be outweighed by the combined benefits of affordability, convenience of location, and gentrification". Wargent said most property investors believed high-crime rates would have a detrimental effect on property price growth, but it was apparent the opposite was often true.

RiskWise Property found that high-crime areas trumped neighbouring suburbs perceived as safer when comparing their five-year growth to the city's median. RiskWise CEO Doron Peleg said, "Our nationwide research actually found gentrifying suburbs with high crime typically deliver strong price growth and outperform the local benchmark", with affordability being the key driver for house price increases. In Sydney, the 10-year capital growth rates for houses in 10 high-crime suburbs analysed by RiskWise materially outperformed the Greater Sydney growth rate, with the weakest performer, Granville, still outperforming the wider-market median price growth by 7%. The results were similar in Melbourne.

At Hotspotting, we wholeheartedly agree. At the start of 2025, I wrote a comprehensive national report for a high-profile national organisation, one of a series that I put together for them, analysing the capital cities and regional markets nationwide. This particular report struck a hurdle: company personnel objected to the inclusion of downmarket suburbs on the lists of recommended places to buy. Nobody, they argued, would want to live in such places. A particular sticking point was the high rating I gave to Wiley Park, a low-end Sydney suburb in the Canterbury-Bankstown LGA. It was deemed to be unsafe and a hotbed for "terrorists"; they couldn't be seen to be recommending such a hellhole. But at a time when Sydney overall was growing only 2% to 3% a year, Wiley Park property values were lifting at an average annual growth rate of 11% (which means values doubling in seven years), well above Sydney market norms. The vacancy rate was 1.2% and rents were rising steadily. Clearly, people wanted to live there, notwithstanding the derision of the real estate snobs. Nearby Lakemba, another stigmatised suburb considered to have social problems, saw house values rise 22% in a year when Sydney overall managed just 2%.

The most ridiculed suburb in the Greater Brisbane area is Inala, considered a hotbed of social problems, where almost half of residents were born overseas. The five-year capital growth average for Inala? It's 17% per year. The median house price increased from $345,000 in 2020 to $750,000 in 2025. Happy is the real estate consumer who ignored the putdowns and bought a humble house there around the time COVID appeared.

The equivalent in the far north of Greater Brisbane is Deception Bay, unkindly dubbed "Inala by the sea". In the 12 months to April 2025, median prices rose 16% for houses and 30% for units. The long-term growth averages were around 15% per year (values doubling in less than five years). In a recent four-year window, the median unit price went from $255,000 to $540,000. The vacancy rate was 0.8% and rents rose 11.4% in 12 months.

The vast municipality that encompasses the south of Greater Brisbane, Logan City, is often referred to as Bogan City. It abounds with downmarket clusters of "don't go there" suburbs with all the usual markers of dysfunction: unemployment, high crime rates and single-parent families. The backyard barbie assessment of buying a small unit there is, "You're kidding, right?" Yet, here's the 12-month growth in median unit prices in mid-2025:

- Loganlea, 27%
- Logan Central, 29%
- Woodridge, 36%
- Beenleigh, 29%
- Kingston, 27%

What does daggy Loganlea offer to the budget buyer or tenant? Proximity to Logan Hospital, Griffith University, two major motorways, trains linking to Brisbane and the Gold Coast, major shopping and schools – and affordability.

The City of Playford in the northern suburbs of Adelaide is arguably the downmarket capital of the nation. It features the Elizabeth suburbs (there are eight of them, named after Queen Elizabeth II, and not because the housing was palatial). Here are the per-year capital growth averages of some of these "slum" areas from 2020 to 2025:

- Elizabeth South, 25.9%
- Elizabeth Park, 21.5%
- Elizabeth East, 22.4%
- Elizabeth North, 25.7%

Over the same period, the median house price for nearby Davoren Park rose from $171,000 to $511,000.

Compare those growth rates to big-city suburbs synonymous with wealth, glamour and prestige, all suburbs with median house prices well above $3 million in 2025:

- Toorak, Vic., 0.6%
- Brighton, Vic., 2.1%
- Manly, NSW, 4.2%

- Bondi Beach, NSW, 9.4%
- Vaucluse, NSW, 7.3%
- Peppermint Grove, WA, 2.1%

I could go on, but you get the idea.

And what do we learn from this? That the reasons why property values rise have little to do with prestige or timeless quality, or proximity to the CBD or swimming pools. It's not about the best streets in the best suburbs. Here's what the Elizabeth suburbs offered to the people who are happy they bought there five years ago: affordability, train links, schools, shopping and proximity to major employment nodes.

If you'd paid $5 million for a house in Toorak in 2020, it would have been worth about the same in 2025. If you'd invested that $5 million in 20 houses in the Elizabeth suburbs in 2020, they'd be worth over $12 million in 2025.

The reality that the downmarket areas are the best performers is a win-win-win situation for buyers at the affordable end of the market: cheaper prices, higher rental yields and superior capital growth.

7. They say you must choose between growth and yield

One of the enduring myths of investment is that you need to make a choice: growth or yield. You can't have both in the same investment.

Wrong.

If you buy real estate in the right places, you can achieve an attractive balance between a good rental yield and strong capital growth. You can have positive cashflow *and* rising values. And you don't have to go downmarket or out west.

There's no doubt that yields are higher on cheaper properties, but you can buy good-quality real estate in good locations and get good rental yields from permanent tenants. You can achieve it in the smaller capital cities and in good regional centres.

Hotspotting publishes a quarterly report called *The Pulse* in conjunction with depreciation experts Washington Brown. It features 50 locations across Australia with above-average capital growth. To weed out high-risk locations like mining towns, we apply additional criteria – the 50 locations must also have credentials for capital growth.

The May 2024 edition demonstrates this well. All the locations on the list had gross rental yields above 6%, with many exceeding 7%, but they were also places where prices were strongly rising. A year later, at a time when the national median price rose just a few percent, the average rate of growth across the 50 selections was 18%, or $91,915. The best individual performer was Aitkenvale, a suburb of Townsville, which rose 40%. Only one of the 50 selections went backwards in value.

ACT TWO
THE MISTAKES

J ames Clear wrote in the global bestseller *Atomic Habits* that having goals is not the key factor – winners and losers often have the same goals. The difference is the habits of those who become winners.

This helps to explain why so many people have unrealised ambitions in real estate investment. People with real estate aspirations make rookie errors, and most never get beyond one property. They have bad habits.

Chapter 4

The case of Gladstone and Moranbah

Imagine spending $600,000 on an investment property and it halves in value. And then that value keeps falling until it's worth only $200,000. And then falls further.

Then, imagine it happens to you with two other similar properties, because you bought three investment properties in the same location and the market collapsed.

I know people who faced that situation.

One couple who contacted me had bought five properties in two high-risk locations and ended up with an entire portfolio worth less than half of what they had paid for it. Their loans were considerably greater than the value of their properties, and rents had fallen through the floor, which meant it was costing them money every week to own properties that were falling in value, and they couldn't sell without losing hundreds of thousands of dollars. They wanted advice on how to rescue the situation. They desperately wanted a solution, but there wasn't one, other than to wait years for those markets to recover and hope they would rise back to the boom levels some time in their lifetime.

This is the stuff of nightmares – if you can even get to sleep as you contemplate your financial future. How could anyone get into so much trouble? How could they make such bad decisions? But people do, in their thousands.

In 2010 it was apparent that the industrial city of Gladstone in central Queensland was facing massive change. Coal seam gas was all the rage, and plants were being built to process this resource into liquefied natural gas (LNG) for export. Three such plants were planned for Gladstone. The total investment was $60 billion, and there would be tens of thousands of jobs during the construction phase. For a regional centre of 60,000 people, this was immense.

Across Australia, thousands of mum-and-dad investors had the same thought: the Gladstone property market was headed for a boom. All those workers would be looking for places to rent or to buy.

For about two years, they appeared to be right. Throughout 2011 and 2012, rents rose and so did property values. The media was writing about Gladstone as the Klondike of the 21st century – a gas rush town where fortunes could be made.

It was around about then, 2012, that I was warning investors to avoid Gladstone. If you already owned there, now was the time to sell – as quickly as you could.

Two things were happening. The first problem was that developers were building new housing estates and apartment blocks – lots of them. Individual developers keen to exploit the boom seemed unaware that hundreds more had the same idea. Too much was being built.

The other problem was that most of the gas plant workers weren't renting local dwellings. The resources companies were building temporary workers camps to house their construction personnel.

The outcome was oversupply.

Oversupply is the dirtiest word in real estate. It's the one thing that can kill a market and cause values to collapse.

In Gladstone, thousands of new dwellings were built for which there was no demand. Vacancies rose above 10%, rents fell and property values headed south. Those who had bought in Gladstone experienced every investor's worst-case scenario: a property worth considerably less than they had paid for it. Those who had bought multiple properties faced a financial calamity.

Not far from Gladstone, in the coal mining town of Moranbah, a similar scenario was in play. For a while, Moranbah was the darling of the property investment world. It had growth rates that investors dream about: in the space of 10 years, the median house price rose from $50,000 to $750,000, growing at an average rate of 30% per year, which is quite extraordinary. For those who got in early and got out before it was too late, it was quite the windfall. However, few people get their timing so right, because few can see what's coming.

At the peak, around 2013, the typical Moranbah house cost $750,000 and rented for $1500 a week. Those were beautiful numbers for the investor-owners but ugly for the big mining companies in the Bowen Basin region, so they developed a new model: they would fly in their workers and accommodate them in temporary workers camps. Fly-in fly-out (FIFO) personnel became the new norm, and suddenly no one had a need for those Moranbah houses – not at any price, but certainly not for $1500 a week.

So, vacancies rose and rents crashed. Inevitably, property values reacted. And then, the resources boom came to a halt, and values fell further. Eventually, in 2018, the typical Moranbah house was worth $150,000. For those who bought at the peak, around $750,000, this was a horror story.

In Western Australia around the same time, the same story evolved in such iconic resources towns as Port Hedland, Karratha and Newman. In Port Hedland, the median house price reached a mind-numbing $1.2 million before falling to around $400,000. In Karratha, houses purchased for $800,000 were worth $300,000. Today, property values in Port Hedland and Karratha are still well below those peak levels in 2013.

Yet, investors still buy in resource centres like Moranbah and Port Hedland, lured by the high rental yields. In May 2025 I wrote a report listing my 20 no-go zones – the high-yield locations I did not recommend. They were all mining towns, resource centres or remote rural towns servicing farming communities. Many offered ultra-cheap houses and yields above 10%. I wrote at the time, "Be afraid, be very afraid".

These case studies illustrate many of the mistakes rookie property investors make. The next chapter will explore those mistakes in detail, but there are key lessons to draw from these stories:

1. Prices do fall, and in some instances they can fall a lot.

2. High-risk locations must be avoided.

3. Buying in good locations is the key message in this book.

Chapter 5

The rookie errors

Here are the main reasons why people fail in real estate investment – the mistakes wannabe investors commonly make.

Rookie error #1: They get the first one wrong

There are several clear reasons why fewer than 1% of property investors have a portfolio and most never get beyond one property. The biggest single reason, though, is that they get the first one wrong. Far too many make one or other of the following rookie errors – or all of them – and mess up their first foray into real estate. Some never recover from that blunder.

Get your first investment property wrong and it can scuttle a 10-year strategy. To succeed with real estate investment, you need the first one to go well. It's critical that it pays its own way, grows in the first year and doesn't use up all your borrowing capacity. Then, it's easier to get finance for the next one, and the third, and all subsequent purchases.

Here's a happy scenario. It's January 2024. You own your home, you have savings, and you decide to buy an investment property. So, you consult your trusted accountant and a recommended mortgage broker. You speak to successful investors and get recommendations for mentors. You pay for quality research information. With the help of your mentor and accountant, you make a plan and develop a 10-year strategy. You establish clear criteria for your first purchase: you will buy a house on land in a regional centre with growth credentials, paying around $500,000 with a rental yield around 6%. You work through your mortgage broker to get pre-approval for a loan, and you engage a recommended buyers' agency with a strong track record of professional service, ethics and success.

Your buyers' agency presents Rockhampton, Queensland, as a worthwhile location because of its affordability, high rental yields and strong growth prospects – it has a strong, diverse economy creating jobs, its population is growing and there's big infrastructure spend happening. So, in March 2024, you buy a house in a Rockhampton suburb for $490,000.

You've selected a good location, and by mid-2025 your property is worth $610,000. You spent around $20,000 on information and advice – from your mentor, accountant, buyers' agent and research reports – but recouped that in the first couple of months' capital growth. Now, you have over $100,000 in equity and are well placed to consider your next investment.

Here's a less joyful case study. It's January 2025. You own your home, you have savings, and you decide to buy an investment property. You've read in the mainstream media that Perth property is raging, and you want to be part of the boom, so you go online and start looking at properties for sale. You've heard that inner-city suburbs close to the CBD are the best options, so that's where you focus. You put in offers on a number of properties, but there's lots of competition from other buyers, and you keep getting outbid by competitors offering higher prices and unconditional contracts.

By May 2025, you're frustrated but remain determined. You've read that the Real Estate Institute of Western Australia (REIWA) says the boom is as strong as ever – prices are still rising 20% a year and are expected to keep going up for several more years. You find another property online with a price guide of $600,000 to $650,000. Based on previous experience of being outbid, you make an offer of $670,000 with an unconditional contract: no finance clause, and no building and pest inspection. Your offer is accepted, and you celebrate, expecting it will be worth $800,000 by mid-2026.

Two months later, you're struggling to find a good tenant at the rent you were told to expect. You didn't realise Perth rental growth had come to a halt a year earlier because so many investors had bought there in the previous two to three years and there was increased supply in the market. You eventually find a tenant, but the rent is less than you were told to expect. The property loses money week after week, and you have to contribute from your salary to pay the mortgage, rates, insurance and maintenance costs.

Another month later, your tenants report serious issues with the hot water system, termite damage and water intrusion causing problems with mould – problems that might have been revealed by a pre-purchase building and pest inspection, but you decided not to do that.

By mid-2026, the property is not worth the $800,000 you expected – it is worth less than you paid for it. You bought after the peak and paid too much, and prices have not grown since. The costs of ownership greatly exceed the rental income, and you have had to spend tens of thousands on repairs and maintenance. Your circumstances don't allow you to buy other properties, and indeed you may have to sell in Perth because of the financial burden. Your property investment journey pretty much ends there.

Rookie error #2: They don't have a plan

I have an eight-step process for succeeding with investing in real estate. Looking for properties to buy is step seven. But that's where most investors start, neglecting steps one to six, which are crucial to success. Those earlier steps are about setting goals, developing a strategy to achieve those goals, understanding your risk profile and your borrowing capacity, creating a team of experts in a range of disciplines and conducting serious research.

Most neglect those early foundational steps in their haste to get to the exciting bit – and jump into property investment without a plan.

Most first-timers don't know what they don't know. Often, what they think they know is questionable. Most people I have interviewed for my podcast *How to Be Part of the 1%* admit their first foray into real estate was a disaster.

The first-time buyer without a strategy might start searching online for somewhere sexy, like Surfers Paradise or Byron Bay, or some other specific location on which they have fixated. Fixation on location is a common syndrome among investors. I get lots of questions from wannabe investors, but nine out of 10 relate to location. "What do you think of Newtown as a place to buy?" "What are your thoughts on Manly?" "Do you think Brighton is a hotspot?"

When I ask why they're focused on that location, the answers include these:

- "I read somewhere it's booming."
- "I live near there and it's a very popular area with tourists."
- "My uncle reckons it's going to take off."
- "It's a prime suburb and they always show the best growth, don't they?"
- "I was there at the weekend and I liked the feel of the place."

If I was marking this as an assignment, they would all be getting an F – or a D-minus if they managed to spell their name correctly.

The answer I'd like to get is along these lines:

> I have a strategy I've developed to achieve my goals with property investment. I'm seeking a property in a particular price range that provides a yield of at least 6% and is located in an area with good growth potential, based on existing and planned infrastructure. This location ticks all the boxes for me, but I was keen to find out what you thought. I don't want to jump in without consulting experts.

I get that response from investors very rarely. Most are acting on an impulse rather than working to a considered plan. This is why so few get to own more than one or two properties.

If you start your investment journey by looking online for properties to buy, you're likely to fail. You're starting in the wrong place, and then you're likely to make matters worse by finishing in the wrong place: buying in a poor location.

Here's just one example of something you should be considering before looking at properties for sale: the buying entity. Should you buy in your own name, in joint names, in a trust, in a company, in a self-managed super fund (SMSF)? There are tax and other implications, and the answer depends on the individual's circumstances. But most don't give it any attention.

Rookie error #3: They're unwilling to invest in knowledge and advice

The most successful investors treat real estate investment as a business, and in business, you have to spend money to make money. It's one of those clichés that's nevertheless true.

My daily encounters with prospective investors reveal that most set out on their property journey with nothing in their kitbag – there's no money set aside for quality research or expert advice. The standard proposition is this: *Yes*, I'll spend $500,000 to buy a property, but *no*, I won't invest $15,000 in a good buyers' agent to find the right property for me, and *no*, I won't spend $1500 on expert advice, and *no*, I won't even spend $150 on a research report to make sure I buy in the right location.

This is the worst kind of false economy. You cannot penny-pinch your way to success in property investment. Smart consumers invest in knowledge and essential advice. Experienced investor and buyers' agent Sanjeev Sah, who I interviewed for my television show *The Property Playbook*, told me he has invested "hundreds of thousands of dollars" in education to ensure he will be successful.

I often say to wannabe investors, "Build your team before you build your portfolio". Your team needs to include:

- an accountant who understands real estate
- a mortgage broker who can find the best finance deals
- a lawyer who specialises in real estate
- a research source with a proven track record (WARNING: newspapers are not research sources)
- a buyers' agent with real life experience (not the thousands who call themselves buyers' agents but have little knowledge and zero track record)
- a mentor with real time spent as an investor
- a quantity surveyor to provide a depreciation report
- ultimately, a property manager recommended by someone who knows who's best.

Research – real research, not tuning into media headlines and soundbites – is fundamentally important. As comedian Ricky Gervais said, "Opinions don't affect facts. But facts should affect opinions, and do, if you're rational". But many people buy in haste and repent at leisure. According to Finder research published by the *Australian Financial Review* in June 2025, 45% of first-time buyers who had bought in the past year regretted their decisions. Regrets included paying too much and buying in the wrong area.

Rookie error #4: They're experts in procrastination

Australia's most awarded buyers' agent, Rich Harvey of Propertybuyer, tells of a colleague he often sees at the gym who always wants to chat to him about his real estate ambitions. For years he has been talking about "getting into the market" but always has a reason why now is not the right time. I can imagine that five years from now, they'll be having the same conversation, and his colleague will have missed repeated opportunities for growth.

For people nervous about taking that big step to spend half a million dollars or more, there's always a seemingly plausible reason to "wait and see". The May 2025 federal election was a great reason to wait and see. Media speculation about interest rates is a popular excuse for procrastination. Economic disruption caused by major global events – the GFC, the COVID pandemic, Donald Trump's tariff war – can be cause for pause. Indeed, the first half of 2025 was a perfect storm of reasons to wait and see.

The reality is that none of these things is a valid reason to put your investment plans on hold. None of them changes the ultimate equation: that real estate is (or should be) a long-term play. Over the period that you own a property there will be fluctuations with the global economy, interest rates and the people in power in Canberra, but none of it alters the fundamental reasons why property values rise.

The greatest example of how procrastination can cost people big money was the media speculation about property prices when COVID hit in early 2020. People who were planning to invest at that time put their plans aside because the mainstream media ran daily stories about the impending collapse of property values. By the time everyone realised the opposite was happening, they had missed out on 20% or more growth in values. For someone who had planned to buy a $600,000 property, hesitating cost them $120,000 or more.

Those driven by knowledge and research would have made different choices and bought at the early stage of an extraordinary boom. I bought in Adelaide in 2020, ignoring the media sensation about the imminent collapse of property values. Within four years, that property had doubled in value.

The bottom line is that "wait and see" people seldom take action and spend a lifetime regretting it – or blaming others for their apathy.

Rookie error #5: They follow the herd

I like this quote from James Clear, author of *Atomic Habits*: "One way to stand out is to look for pockets of low competition … People are drawn to where it is crowded. Look for the quiet spaces inside your areas of interest. Excellence often hides at the edges".

This is highly relevant to Australian real estate. However, in real estate, most people do the opposite: they follow the pack. They like the crowded places.

It's natural for people to be herd animals. There's comfort in being part of a pack of like-minded persons. There's reassurance in the belief that if everyone's doing something, it must be the right way. That may work in some areas of human existence, but not in real estate investment.

In real estate, the opposite is what works. The people who think and act independently (and sensibly) are the ones who succeed in real estate investment. But they're in the minority. And this is why relatively few Australians achieve outstanding success in property investment. Most like the comfort of the herd, but no one ever got rich following the herd. Success belongs not to the pack animal but to the lone wolf.

But being part of the pack feels safer and easier. It's difficult to be the lone wolf. Difficult, but essential if you want to do well in real estate.

The problem with herds is that they're not driven by logic or reason. Herds are skittish and prone to panic. However, many people would prefer to be part of a herd that's stampeding towards a cliff than be the strong-minded individual who detaches from the rampaging pack and heads in the opposite direction.

There's plenty of evidence that people who reject the herd have the greatest success with investment. One of the world's leading investors, Warren Buffett – the fifth wealthiest human in 2025, with a net worth of US$160 billion – has always preached an anti-herd approach. "Sell when others are buying, and buy when others are selling" is his simple mantra.

In 2020, when COVID struck, investors collectively were not adopting the Warren Buffett philosophy. They were milling around in the herd waiting for a signal that it was time to attack. Most of the media signals advised retreat.

First-home buyers and other owner-occupiers were busy in the market, taking advantage of high levels of government assistance, low interest rates and busy activity in specific markets. Their activity was putting upward pressure on prices in many locations across Australia. But investors were mostly inactive, and they were missing opportunities to buy well for future growth.

And then, early in 2021, the herd began to stampede. The media began to write about a property boom, and investors piled into the market. It became a frenzy, with many buyers paying too much. The well-researched minority had bought six to 12 months earlier because they knew it was coming.

That's also what happened when investors and developers piled into the Gladstone market from 2010 to 2012, when the big gas plants were being built. Those who bought multiple properties and ended up with assets worth less than their loans were herd animals. They did no research. They did not consult independent experts. They just stampeded along with the rest of the pack.

In 2021 and 2022 my Hotspotting business started recommending locations in Perth in our *National Top 10 Best Buys* report. There was pushback from consumers who challenged our reasons for recommending a city that had experienced falling property values for most of the previous decade. Our rationale was simple: things were changing for Perth, and we believed it would become a national growth leader. By 2024 Perth was indeed the national leader on price, and the media was full of stories about the Perth boom. Buyers were clamouring to be part of it, paying silly prices for poor properties without doing the usual due diligence. Thousands paid too much for bad real estate at the peak of the boom. Such is life for the herd animals.

The smart money had bought two or three years earlier. All power to the independent thinkers.

As Steven Pressfield writes in *The War of Art*, "The human being isn't wired to function as an individual. We're wired tribally, to act as part of a group ... we know how to fit into the band and the tribe. What we don't know is how to be alone. We don't know how to be free individuals".

I repeat: no one ever got rich following the herd. Some have succeeded by leading the herd, but in real estate you get the best results by leaving the herd completely.

Rookie error #6: They react to media soundbites

Successful investing is built on research. And research can be hard work and involve a great many things. Here's what it doesn't involve: making big-money decisions based on media soundbites.

Every data release from research sources usually contains some positives and some negatives, but the media will usually focus on the negatives. For example, throughout most of 2020, data on vacancy rates had been overwhelmingly positive for property markets, with most capital cities and regional centres having very tight rental markets, putting upward pressure on rents and prices. But mainstream media, seeking to milk the pandemic for clickbait headlines, focused on the small number of negative figures, such as the high level of vacancies in inner-city areas. So, the soundbiters had been getting lots of sour messages, including predictions since March 2020 that markets were on the point of collapse, with property values set to fall 20% or 30%.

In October, seven months after those dire forecasts were first made, we were yet to see any evidence of it. Of the 15 market jurisdictions in Australia, 11 had house prices higher than at the start of the year, according to CoreLogic data. But most investors continued to mill around the fringes of the market, waiting for some signal that it was time for the next bull run.

I wrote at the time, "Most of them will stampede into the market when they hear there's a boom happening. And that means they will miss the best time to buy. Many of them will buy at the peak and will potentially lose money". And that's what happened in early 2021. The FOMO (fear of missing out) syndrome, the worst motivation for buying property, took over.

I state several times in this book that real estate coverage is riddled with misinformation. The standard of reporting on markets and issues is pitifully bad. Most of it constitutes recycled press releases from people with a vested interest in the message – it's propaganda, not news. And most reporting on real estate issues is conducted by people with little or no experience of property ownership.

The increasing use of AI exacerbates the problem. Treating ChatGPT as a search engine merely invites the AI to regurgitate all the media misinformation on real estate. When I'm asked about the keys to success in property investment, I often begin my answer like this: "Rule one: stop reading newspapers".

The Perth market in the first half of 2025 provides a case study. All the evidence from independent research provided an emphatic conclusion: the Perth boom had passed its peak. All the data sources agreed that Perth was no longer leading on price growth. The days of 20%-plus annual growth were over. But the news media continued to publish articles declaring that the boom was raging on. Vested interests – including REIWA, the body that represents real estate agents in Perth – were transmitting press releases proclaiming a boom without end, and journalists were waving them through to your newsfeed without expert scrutiny. This self-serving propaganda was being presented to consumers as fact. A buyer who acted on that distortion of the truth risked losing a lot of money.

Rookie error #7: They buy locally

A clear-thinking real estate consumer who has researched well should always get a happy result. Australia is a vast country, and there is so much choice – so many good places to live and so many fine options for investment.

I'm often asked, "Is this a good time to buy?" My standard answer is, "That's the wrong question. It's always a good time to buy somewhere in Australia. The right question is, 'Where is it a good time to buy?'"

In this vast nation, with so many different scenarios playing out at any point in time, there are always options to buy well in locations with good future prospects. A smart buyer will consider all of Australia as their market.

But not every buyer is smart. Many want to buy an investment property in their own backyard. The rationale is usually one of these three options:

1. I know my local market.
2. If I look interstate, I won't be able to check it out myself before buying.
3. I want to be able to drive by regularly and check on it.

All those rationales are irrational.

They know their local market? I'm certain the average punter making that claim can't answer any of these questions:

- What's the median house price in this suburb, and how does it compare to its neighbours?
- What's the local vacancy rate?
- What's the median rent for a two-bedroom unit?
- What's the average "days on market"?
- How much have prices risen in the past 12 months and the past five years?
- What percentage of property is owned by investors?
- What are the key drivers of prices in this area?

They want to inspect the property before they buy? I never have. There's no point. I'm not an electrician, or a plumber, or a builder. Most of the things I need to be concerned about are hidden, or visible only to expert eyes. I want skilled specialists to look for me – a buyers' agent, a local property manager, a building and pest inspector. There's nothing to be gained from a personal viewing. I can use all the online tools to check out the area, the street and the property itself, and pay professionals to check out the structure.

They want to drive by and check on it? What will that reveal? When you buy an investment property, you appoint a local property manager with good credentials, and it's their job to check on it with regular inspections, followed by a detailed report with photos. In over 40 years of owning real estate, I've never had a problem – except when I've tried to self-manage.

Rookie error #8: They buy in one-industry markets

Economic diversity is an essential ingredient of a growth location, especially from a long-term perspective – and investors should always take a long-term view. There will be a lot more about that later in the book.

One-horse towns may have growth spurts, but they are usually unsustainable. Queensland coal mining town Moranbah had startling growth for a heady period, but ultimately, its market collapsed. Port Hedland values soared to dizzying heights during the resources investment boom, but when that ended, the market went south. Those who bought at the peak may never recover financially. This kind of volatility is the norm for single-sector economies like mining towns; they are not for the weak of heart, nor for the smart of brain.

I've never met anyone who claimed to have conducted thorough research and concluded that buying real estate in a resources town was the best option, but I have spoken to many who dived in because they heard there was a boom and they didn't want to miss out.

Another common one-industry scenario that lures the unwary is tourism. Some of Australia's most iconic locations are tourist towns. They attract short-term visitors and retirees. They seldom produce sustainable long-term growth. Tourism is fickle and vulnerable to economic shocks or bad weather. It's discretionary spending. If people are worried about the economy or their jobs, they'll cut the expensive holiday.

The recent history of Byron Bay provides a case study. The median house price more than doubled in two years when the COVID boom meshed with the trend I have dubbed the "exodus to affordable lifestyle". Once that feeding frenzy was satisfied, values went dramatically south. Values rose 145% from May 2020 to June 2022 (from $1.425 million to $3.5 million), then dropped 33% between November 2022 and October 2023 (to $2.36 million, more than $1 million below the peak); within a year it was back up to $3.5 million, but then it quickly dropped to $2.6 million. This kind of extreme volatility is unusual in real estate – it occurs only in one-industry economies. If you enjoy roller coasters, this is the place to buy.

Noosa and the Sunshine Coast provide a similar case study, but with a happy ending. Noosa has long been an iconic holiday destination and property market, but prior to 2020 it had a terrible track record on capital growth. It was a one-industry location, vulnerable to downturns. But that changed in the early years of the 2020s. How? A massive program of infrastructure development in the Sunshine Coast broadened and strengthened the regional economy and brought new residents to the region. In June 2025, most Sunshine Coast and Noosa suburbs had five-year capital growth averages in the 12% to 15% per year range, including iconic Noosa Heads. A 15% growth average means values are doubling within five years.

A third type of location with high vulnerability is country towns where the economy depends on agriculture. These locations can be devastated by drought and bushfires – or dummy spits by nations who buy Australian produce. Sometimes – including during the COVID boom, when some buyers were targeting anywhere cheap – they attract a buyer feeding frenzy. Hamilton in far western Victoria is one example among many: its median house price rose from $230,000 in mid-2020 to $385,000 two years later, but over the next three years prices flatlined. In a May 2025 report to clients, I highlighted some of the country towns in Queensland and New South Wales where house prices had dropped in the previous 12 months:

- Hughenden, 41%
- Clermont, 8%
- Moura, 15%
- Coonabarabran, 12%
- Coonamble, 35%

Hughenden's median house price dropped below $100,000 and Coonamble was down to $165,000. I commented, "These locations are cheap for a reason".

Mining towns, tourism towns and country towns have a lot in common. They are one-industry economies. Their real estate markets sometimes have growth spurts, but the growth is not sustainable. Long-term, they don't deliver. And far too often, they are a graveyard for investors' money.

Rookie error #9: They put all their nest-eggs in the one basket

Diversity is a key word in property investment. Buying in places that offer economic diversity is important.

As you build a property portfolio, diversifying your holdings geographically is also crucial. Remember the earlier example of the investor who owned five properties, all in Gladstone and Moranbah, when that boom evaporated.

Many people would love to own 10 investment properties, but imagine someone who owned 10 properties in 2024, all in Victoria. Victoria has at times been a national leader of economic, population and property growth, but in the 2020s it was a noted underachiever, particularly from 2022 to 2025, when other markets were thriving. This investor would have been feeling sick about their situation during that period; their portfolio might have been worth $5 million in 2020 but $4 million in 2025, and the state's high property taxes and draconian rental laws would have caused a major drain on day-to-day finances.

If that investor was patient and able to ride out the tough times, the future might be brighter. But it's never smart to put all your nest-eggs in the one economic basket. That's for basket cases.

If those 10 properties had been spread throughout other major cities, the owner would have enjoyed some capital growth. Over the period when Melbourne was declining, Brisbane, Perth, Adelaide, the Gold Coast and many other locations had booming values.

There's a second reason why spreading your risk across multiple states and territories is smart: you can avoid paying land tax. This insidious impost is a state tax: if you own six properties in Queensland, you'll be paying lots of land tax, but if you own six properties in six different states, you'll probably be paying no land tax – or very little – because you are likely to be below a state's land tax threshold with just one property.

Rookie error #10: They trade rather than accumulate

Warren Buffett, who I mentioned earlier as a proponent of not following the herd, also advocates taking a long-term view of investment. He buys good assets with the intention of keeping them. He's an accumulator, not a trader. He says he doesn't care if they shut the market and it doesn't reopen for five years, because he has no intention of selling the good assets he owns. In a letter to shareholders of his company Berkshire Hathaway Inc., he wrote, "our favourite holding period is forever".

I was once interviewed by a real estate podcaster who asked everyone the same question: "What advice would you give the 25-year-old?"

My answer was short and to the point: "Never ever sell".

Had I understood that simple philosophy in my 20s, I would still have the first property I owned: a house I bought for $25,000 in the early 1980s, which is now worth around $700,000. I would still own the second home I bought at a cost of $50,000: a humble house sited on an elevated block with majestic views and today worth over $1 million for the land alone.

All the truly successful investors I have known have this in common: they're collectors. They understand the value of a growing portfolio with equity that can fund further purchases. They also understand that when you sell, you lose a lot of your gains to capital gains tax, agents' commissions and other selling costs.

Rookie error #11: They sell too soon

The oldest cliché in real estate, and the truest, is that it's a long-term play. Time in the market is more important than timing the market. Yet, many fail to comprehend the truth in that statement. They get into the market, stay a year or two, then get out.

Many did that in 2024 and 2025 because the costs of ownership were unsustainable. Despite very high rents, the income was less than the total cost of being a landlord, including loan payments, council rates, insurance, land tax, and repairs and maintenance. In 2024 investment properties cost more to own than they earned for 65% of landlords, up from 57% the year before, according to the *PIPA Annual Property Investor Sentiment Survey 2024*.

Others cash in after a couple of years of good capital growth, eager to spend the profits. That can be short-sighted and, ultimately, counterproductive.

In 2025 the Australian Housing and Urban Research Institute (AHURI) published a study on the behaviour of landlords. Its most surprising finding was that many investor-owners sell after only a few years of ownership. In fact, the study found that 22% of rental properties are sold after only one year, and half of investment properties are sold within two years. Those who sell quickly are usually in the 25 to 34 age group and are likely to have fewer financial resources than those who hold their properties for longer.

As I mentioned earlier, the philosophy I've developed in my 40-plus years in real estate analysis is this: never ever sell. Buy good assets and keep them. Accumulate.

However, valuer and experienced investor Gavin Hegney says there's another viewpoint: "Sometimes you have to sell to realise your gains", he says. "How do you turn a really good investment into an average investment? Hang on to it for too long."

Rookie error #12: They switch off after purchase

Hotspotting has memberships that provide all our research reports and access to an online portal with an array of information tools for real estate consumers who understand the importance of staying informed. When a membership comes up for renewal, we sometimes we get this response: "Oh, I don't need it anymore because I've already bought something".

This is a fairly standard mentality that many people would understand. Why should you research the market if you've already purchased a property and don't plan to buy again in the near future?

The Gladstone case study described earlier provides one answer. People got caught because they stopped paying attention. When they bought, the market was rising. They settled the purchase and then relaxed. By the time they realised the market had gone into reverse, and their property's value was falling, it was too late for many of them to take action. Had they stayed connected, they would have realised what was coming. At the time, I was warning people of the imminent decline, but if you weren't getting our emails to members – or otherwise staying up to date – you would not have known about it.

If you're a serious investor and your goal is to grow a property portfolio, you can never switch off and tune out. You must stay in touch and keep informed.

The other end of this problem arises when the investor who bought a first property and then switched off decides it's time to buy property number two. Usually, that would be one or two years after finalising the first. If they've paid no attention to market trends in the interim, they're restarting from a position of ignorance.

ACT THREE
THE
ANSWERS

Guy Williams has two businesses. As his day job, he runs a successful Sydney corporate training business. His second business is property investment. He built a portfolio of 38 residential properties by the age of 55. He could retire and do adventure tourism, which is one of his passions – he's done Everest, Kilimanjaro, the Camino and the Kokoda Trail – but he doesn't, because he loves his day job and his second business, property investing. He just keeps doing what he enjoys.

There are a number of things that explain his success. He started early and kept going. He based his decisions on research. He built a team of trusted advisers, and he's willing to pay for their services.

He was a Premium Member of Hotspotting for many years, and he has also bought information from other sources. In other words, he does serious research. He has mentors and advisers, and he is always willing to invest in knowledge and advice.

His portfolio is broad and diversified, and includes properties in every state and territory. He's done it the right way. The key is that he sees property investment as a business, and he knows he has to spend money to make money. To do otherwise is folly. He says, "It's foolish to spend so much on a property but not be willing to spend any money on research and advice".

Anthony Schiafone doesn't own 40 properties. Not yet. He may do one day. He's younger than Guy Williams – still in his late 30s – and he's made a good start. He owns seven residential properties so far. All are in good locations, all have grown in value and all provide good rental returns. Recently, he sold for $620,000 a property for which he paid $295,000. Now, he's buying small commercial properties.

He's done this on an average wage. He's a government-employed electrician. He is testimony to what can be achieved if you start young and buy smart using sound principles. You don't need a massive income or a university degree.

Anthony has always invested in information and education. He has paid to attend seminars, he buys research information, and he pays respected professionals to mentor him. He has a team of professionals he goes to for advice about finance, legal matters, research and property selection. He's always looking to learn. I recently saw him at a Melbourne seminar on property investment at which I was a speaker.

Guy Williams and Anthony Schiafone are part of that 1% of property investors who have a property portfolio. They've made it their business to understand how real estate works and how to select good locations. They have applied sound business principles to real estate investing and have succeeded.

Read on to find out how you can be like them.

Chapter 6

Starting off on the right foot

In the previous chapter, I explained that the biggest mistake a rookie property investor can make is to start off on the wrong foot. As you prepare to dive in, here are some aspects of your approach you need to get right to avoid making that mistake.

It's a business, not a hobby

Most Australians treat property investment as a hobby. They have limited success. Some experience financial disasters.

Successful investors treat it as a business, and that, in essence, is the difference. With a business, you need to spend money to make money.

Those who regard investment as a hobby seek to do it on the cheap. They will attend a free seminar run by a spruiker, but they won't spend $50 or $100 on an event offered by a recognised expert. They will grab free information published in the media (much of it recycled press release material – that is, propaganda), but they won't spend money on in-depth analysis. They'll miss out on thousands of dollars of tax savings because they refuse to spend a few hundred dollars on a depreciation schedule, or cost themselves thousands because they didn't see a lawyer or accountant before buying in the wrong entity.

I've had conversations with people who are preparing to buy property costing over $500,000 and refuse to spend any money on an independent valuation to make sure they're buying at the right price, or on a building and pest inspection to ensure there are no hidden nasties. They will self-manage a property to avoid paying a fee to a qualified property manager who understands the ever-changing legal landscape. They won't invest any time or money on research, and instead they buy on a whim or a media soundbite.

This is the essence of a hobby investor. They think they're being smart by avoiding expenses or getting things done cheaply, but their refusal to spend small amounts may end up costing them $50,000 or $100,000 because they paid too much, or they didn't realise the house had structural issues, or they were unaware that an easement impacts their property.

This is the difference between the amateur and the professional – and between failure and success.

Build a team before you build a portfolio

You have to put together a team of qualified advisers before you get to work building a property portfolio. As discussed, if you're approaching this the right way, you'll see it as a business. You should register a business name, just to show you're serious, and create a business plan. It doesn't need to be vast – it can be a single page – but it should clearly set out your goal and your plan for achieving it, preferably with input from a mentor.

As an aside, if you have a strategy for real estate, it's smart to stick to it. I have conducted many mentoring sessions with people who have clearly defined their plan for how they will proceed, only to be distracted by a bright, shiny object that has blipped on their radar screen, such as an off-the-plan apartment in a proposed high-rise complex with ocean views.

You need to speak to a range of experts to get the answers to questions like these:

- How much can I borrow?
- How do I feel about risk?
- Should I buy in my own name or my partner's, or through a company, or a trust, or an SMSF?
- How big a part can depreciation claims play in my bottom line?
- How do I determine the right locations to fit my strategy?
- Where do I find the information that will inform my choices?

So, you need to speak to a mortgage broker. It doesn't cost anything to have a chat, and it's important to find out your borrowing capacity before you waste time searching for properties you can't afford.

You need to speak to an accountant. If you don't already have one, ask for recommendations from people you respect. An accountant who understands real estate investment is ideal – not all of them do. There are tax implications to be considered.

You should speak to a lawyer – a real estate specialist – long before you get anywhere near a purchase contract. They cost money, of course, but which is worse: spending a few hundred or even a few thousand on really good advice, or making a rookie mistake that costs you tens of thousands? Buying property in the wrong entity can be costly.

You need to speak to a quantity surveyor who knows about depreciation. You can end up saving thousands of dollars on your tax return if you spend a few hundred dollars on a depreciation schedule.

You need to determine the best sources of research information. To access the best information, you will need to spend some money, but not much relative to the price of real estate. My Hotspotting business is based on providing research-based reports on good places to buy.

Everyone who has succeeded in any field of endeavour has had mentors. Speak to work colleagues or family members and find people who have been successful property investors. Ask them lots of questions. If you can't find anyone in your orbit, the Hotspotting business provides mentoring services.

As you speak to these people, you start to build a team. And you have to be willing to pay for it. Don't be a cheapskate. I regularly speak to people who feel they're not successful unless they get everything at a discount. They want to haggle over the price of everything. My advice: save your haggling energy for getting your next property at the right price.

A smart alternative is to engage an experienced buyers' agent, someone with knowledge and experience. They can help you find the right property in the right location at a price that saves you more than their fee.

If you're not willing to spend some money on good advice, forget about property investment. You're wasting your time, and you'll ultimately waste big money by buying badly.

The key word is "growth"

If you read about property investment, the word you'll encounter most frequently is "growth". It's all about growth.

The *PIPA Annual Investor Sentiment Survey 2020* asked the key question, "Why invest in property?" For 62% of respondents, the answer was long-term capital growth.

Simply put, it means values rise over time – if you buy right. Some locations have grown at an average rate of 10% per year over the past decade. When prices grow at 10% per year, values double in seven years.

Sometimes specific locations experience insane growth. In the early part of the 2020s, some Sunshine Coast suburbs doubled in three years. During the COVID boom, when ridiculous things happened in real estate, Byron Bay doubled in 18 months. Downmarket Adelaide suburbs have doubled in four or five years recently.

More common are places with a long-term growth rate of 7% or 8% per year, which means values are doubling in nine or 10 years – still not a bad result for the owner.

Some locations perform poorly. Their growth rates are just 2% or 3% per year. At 3% per year, it takes 24 years for values to double. And then, there are places where values show no growth over time or even lose value. Apartments in inner-city Melbourne and in iconic Surfers Paradise showed little or no growth in the 10 years to 2020, and median prices were the same or similar to a decade earlier.

Some of the nation's best-known mining towns have property values today that are considerably lower than they were 15 years ago. Port Hedland and Karratha in Western Australia fall into that category, as do Mount Isa and Moranbah in Queensland.

The key is understanding why prices rise strongly in some places, only moderately in others and not at all in the worst performers.

Chapter 7

Understanding the Australian context

Here's how you begin to understand Australian property prices: toss out everything you think you know. Acknowledge that most of what you believe comes from news media, and most of what newspapers and television tell you is suspect. Start with a blank canvas.

I speak to Australian audiences often at conferences, seminars, webinars and live social media broadcasts, as well as through phone calls, emails and Zoom meetings. There are always lots of questions. Most of those questions arise from misinformation.

Here's an example: "Everyone knows the prime inner-city suburbs show the best growth, so what can you do if you can't afford to buy there?"

Here's another: "Given that property doubles in value every 10 years, why does it matter where you buy?"

But perhaps the question that's most common and best proves the average punter has no clue is this one: "Where's the best place to buy right now?"

When people ask questions like that, they think there's a right answer. There isn't – the answer depends on the individual and their circumstances. If 10 people asked that question, there might be 10 different correct answers. In fact, for each individual, there may be five right answers, or 10, or 20.

If you don't understand that, reread the introduction to this chapter. Start with a blank canvas.

Shortage – the imbalance between supply and demand

Any regular supermarket shopper knows how much the price of food items can fluctuate. Apart from the machinations of the big supermarket chains that dominate the food market and are happy to rip off consumers while running television promos about how much they care, there are the vagaries of supply and demand to consider. Demand for food items is fairly constant, but supply can be impacted by weather events, or disease, or a locust plague.

Real estate is considerably more complex, but supply and demand issues are still relevant – particularly in the 2020s, when shortage is a core issue. The "housing crisis" is discussed every day in the media, and the most common conclusion is that there's a rental shortage because we're not building enough homes and there are too few landlords. Residential vacancy rates have been hovering at around 1% nationally since 2021. The industry benchmark for a balanced market with a good supply of rental properties and stable rents is 3% – history shows that this gives tenants a good range of choices and stable rents – but Australia hasn't seen vacancy rates that high in 20 years.

When bank economists forecast falling property values at the start of both 2023 and 2024, they believed high interest rates were the big factor. One reason they were wrong was that the all-pervading shortage of dwellings was a far bigger factor.

Australian consumers continued to demand real estate in an undersupplied market. As I write this in 2025, there is no solution in the foreseeable future. Our political leaders are clueless about how to deal with it. The 2025 federal election confirmed all major parties were bereft of ideas or even the most basic understanding of the problem.

Anthony Albanese's favourite real estate soundbite – we're building 1.2 million new homes in five years – is a cruel hoax. They will fall hundreds of thousands of dwellings short of the target. As a result, there will continue to be upward pressure on dwelling values for many more years.

Why politicians want high property values

Every politician with a position of leadership in state or federal governments has mouthed the usual platitudes about housing affordability. They all care deeply, apparently. Many have promised to fix it. None have succeeded. From what I have observed, none have even tried.

The debate about housing affordability across Australia has filled newspapers and other forms of media with easy content for decades. As mentioned in the introduction to this book, concerns about young Australians being locked out of home ownership have been expressed every year since the 1960s and 1970s, and even as far back as the early years of the 20th century.

Given the high level of concern in the community about high dwelling values and the constant political chatter about it, it's curious that the problem only ever gets worse. Why is this, when the Prime Minister claims he cares about housing affordability and wants to fix it, and every state and territory government leader has said the same? Because they're lying.

There's an argument to be made that politicians want property values to stay high. One reason is that many of them have property portfolios. Another is that high property values mean more government revenue. The core property taxes – council rates, state stamp duty, state land tax and the federal government's capital gains tax – bring in over $100 billion every year. Real estate provides government coffers with the ultimate form of bracket creep. It's cocaine to governments.

Most policy decisions that claim to respond to affordability issues put additional upward pressure on property values. None of the state and federal budgets delivered in 2025 included measures to improve housing affordability or reduce housing costs. They all had schemes to make it a little easier for young buyers to get into the market, thereby fuelling demand, but none to deal with the core issues of high prices, high construction costs and high rents.

James Kirby wrote in *The Australian* in June 2025, "A new generation of property buyers risks paying too much for a first home as a torrent of government incentives hits the market". He referenced the Queensland government's scheme that allows a buyer with a deposit of just 2 per cent to purchase a $1 million home and the federal government's "First Home Guarantee" scheme, for which any first-home buyer automatically qualifies, where most buyers would need only a 5 per cent deposit.

Veteran property analyst Cameron Kusher, formerly of CoreLogic and more recently PropTrack, called these schemes that encourage more people to buy at high prices "a slippery slope". He may have a point. The political leaders who claim to care about affordability are actively making it worse by feeding price growth.

The high cost of new dwellings underpins the value of existing ones

There's a factor no one in politics is dealing with that reinforces the high value of existing dwellings: the cost of building new homes is high. Ridiculously, obscenely high. In 2025, according to the official data, the cost of creating a new house-and-land package in our capital cities was scarily close to $1 million. The median price of a residential block in our capital cities was around $420,000, and the average cost of building a standard brick-and-tile house was $530,000.

The key piece of information is this: between 40% and 50% of that $950,000 cost of a city house-and-land package is taxes, fees and charges at the three levels of government. Young Australians can't afford to build their dream home because the Great Australian Dream is being taxed to death. Many builders and developers are not proceeding with projects for which they have approvals because the costs are prohibitive.

Home-building is also being hampered by bureaucracy. The Productivity Commission found in a 2025 report that it takes twice as long as to create a new home now as it did 30 years ago. The report itemised a series of reasons for this startling lack of advancement in building efficiency, and most of them could be summarised in one word: bureaucracy. Long delays in getting approvals and political tinkering with the design of homes add constantly to cost. Today, we have new dwellings that are safer, more accessible, more energy efficient and more aesthetically pleasing than 20 or 30 years ago, but they cost hundreds of thousands of dollars more to build.

We have the biggest homes on the planet

Australians agonise over housing affordability and the high cost of constructing homes, yet we insist on homes that are larger than we need. Most of our households contain no more than two people – 26% are one-person households and 34% are two-person households – but anything less than four bedrooms and two bathrooms is considered subpar.

Indeed, the World Population Review 2025 found that Australia has the largest homes on the planet. The global average for dwellings is around 100 square metres; the Australian average is more than double that at 214 square metres, compared to 201 in the USA, 181 in Canada, 83 in Sweden, 81 in Italy and just 76 in the UK.

Australians move house a lot

My home in Maleny is my forever home. When my wife Kim and I first saw it, we knew we'd be moving in and staying for good. It suits us brilliantly in every way. We had hoped to buy it for less than the asking price, but another couple also loved it. That competition between two eager buyers pushed up the price.

All it takes for a property's price to rise is two hopefuls vying to buy it. Most buyers hope to get the targeted property for under the list price, but it takes only one other motivated buyer to create competition and ensure that the price will be elevated. When there are multiple committed buyers, properties often sell for considerably more than expected.

Real estate is the only commodity you can buy – with the possible exception of art and antiques – where every item is essentially unique, and potential buyers are placed in direct competition and have to outbid each other to secure that unique item. It doesn't happen that way (usually) when you buy a car, or a lounge suite, or clothes, or supermarket items.

These factors are exacerbated when there's a chronic national shortage of the highly prized commodity.

One key factor putting pressure on this situation is the frequency with which Australians move house. An analysis of ABS data by veteran researcher Michael Matusik in April 2025 found that over 40% of Australian households changed addresses in the previous five years. Some cohorts move a lot more often, with "young" first-home buyers the most restless – 82% had moved at least once in the past five years, with 28% moving once, 19% moving twice and 35% moving three times. In comparison, 57% of older first-home buyers had moved at least once in the past five years. Among the other groupings, a third of "upgraders" moved at least once in the past five years, while a quarter of downsizers moved at least once.

Matusik reported many and varied reasons for home owners moving house. Around three-quarters of moves were driven by the need or desire for housing that was better, bigger or just different. Lifestyle was an important driver, with households seeking nice suburbs, better schools or a sea or tree change. Work-related moves were common – about 30% of interstate relocations were motivated by jobs or careers. All of these motivations are aspirational in nature and, when the people moving end up in competition with other hopefuls, provide impetus for prices to rise.

However, one of the big motivations recently has been cost of living and a desire to reduce expenses. This has been a driver for people leaving the two biggest cities and relocating to regional areas, which offer more affordable housing and a different lifestyle, often enabled by the ability to work remotely. Even with the high cost of selling, buying elsewhere and locating, people are ahead if they sell a big city home for $1.3 million and buy a regional home of similar quality for $800,000. I had that experience in the 1990s when I sold a modest Brisbane home on a small suburban block and bought a renovated Queenslander cottage on acreage with ocean views in a hill-change town, and had money left over.

Chapter 8

What matters most about location

Locations that outperform the market averages have common qualities. I've made a particular study of them for the past 20 years – ever since I wrote a series of feature articles on the subject for *Money* magazine, out of which evolved the Hotspotting business.

It's apparent that the notion of an "Australian property market" driven by interest rate trends and consumer confidence is nonsense. There are more complex forces in play, and an understanding of them explains why we typically have, at any point in time, four different market scenarios happening in different parts of the country:

1. strongly rising prices
2. moderately rising prices
3. stagnating prices (an annual change of less than 1%)
4. declining prices.

Each of those four broad scenarios is evident somewhere in Australia at any point in time, despite the existence of just one official interest rate for the whole nation, a single consumer price index (CPI) reading and lines and lines of economists and journalists declaring that Australian house prices "rose 0.3% last month" or "will decline 6% in the next year". These declarations are the refuge of people too lazy to develop a more sophisticated understanding of the dynamics of property markets.

This was the state of play on 2 September 2024 regarding the growth in median house prices in the previous 12 months, according to CoreLogic:

- **Strongly rising prices:** Perth, 24.3%; regional Western Australia, 19.6%; Adelaide, 14.5%; Brisbane, 14.1%; regional Queensland 12.3%.

- **Moderately rising prices:** Regional South Australia, 9.8%; Sydney, 5.7%; Darwin, 2.9%; Canberra, 2.6%; regional New South Wales, 3.9%; regional Tasmania, 1.4%.

- **Stagnating prices:** regional Victoria, −0.9%; regional Northern Territory, −0.3%.

- **Declining prices:** Melbourne, −1.1%; Hobart, −2.0%.

What did the news media report at the time? That Australian house prices rose 0.5% in August, because that was the average result of all those different performances. The reality is that nowhere in Australia did house prices rise 0.5%. The key fact is that house prices increased in 11 of the 15 market jurisdictions and fell only marginally in the others.

Keep in mind that at the start of 2024, bank economists forecast that prices would fall 10% to 15% across Australia over the coming year because interest rates were high. Someone with an inquiring mind – as you might think a senior economist at a big bank would be – might wonder:

- How do they get their forecasts so wrong every year?

- If the deciding factor is high interest rates, how can prices be booming in some cities, rising only marginally in others and falling in others?

However, as Winston Churchill observed, "Men occasionally stumble over the truth, but most of them pick themselves up and hurry off as if nothing had happened". We can today slightly adjust the quote, because these days many senior economists are women.

The EMPIRICAL formula

My study of the core qualities that cause these stark differences has been a crusade of sorts. I have distilled those key qualities into a process I call "the EMPIRICAL formula". Empirical evidence relies on practical experience rather than theories, and in this case, EMPIRICAL is an acronym. Here's what it means:

- Economy: must be strong and diverse
- Market size: must have a minimum of 50 house sales in the past 12 months
- Population: the LGA ideally would have a population above 15,000
- Infrastructure: good existing amenities and evidence of investment in major new projects
- Rental market: low vacancies likely to put upward pressure on rents
- Increasing employment opportunities: evidence of jobs growth locally
- Capital growth: strong sales activity pointing to future price rises

- Affordability: median house prices below a benchmark level
- Low risk: avoid volatile markets.

Let's examine each of those in greater detail, because together they comprise the secret sauce of why some locations outperform on price.

Economy – must be strong and diverse

Diversity is the key word. There must be multiple industry sectors creating economic activity and jobs.

Townsville in Far North Queensland is one of Australia's strongest regional economies: tourism, manufacturing, resources, education, government administration and the military all have a major impact. It's a key reason Townsville was a national leader in price growth from 2023 to 2025. The Sunshine Coast evolved from an underachiever to a national leader in price growth after its transition from tourist town to multifaceted economy.

Single-industry economies like mining towns, tourist towns and small rural towns seldom produce sustainable long-term price growth. Avoid them, no matter what the temptation might be.

Market size – must have a minimum of 50 house sales in the past 12 months

Wildly distorted price data sometimes gets featured in the mainstream media with allegations that specific locations have had amazing price growth in the previous year. Invariably, this is dodgy data, because these locations are small towns or suburbs with too few sales to give a reliable median price, and the growth figure is bogus. If there are fewer than 50 sales in a year, the market (and the economy on which it is based) is too small to have substance.

Population – the LGA ideally would have a population above 15,000

To generate critical mass as an economy and substance as a property market, the municipality or regional centre needs to have a reasonable population size. My preference is a minimum of 50,000 to have greater comfort that the community can be a generator of growth, but smaller centres have been among the national price-growth champions in recent years, including Warwick and Kingaroy in Queensland. The key factor is the population of the LGA: Kingaroy had a population around 11,000 in 2024 but the LGA of which it is the main town, South Burnett, had 35,000 residents. Oakey is a town of less than 5000, but it punches above its weight because it's part of the Toowoomba City LGA, which with a 2024 population around 185,000 makes it Australia's second largest inland city after Canberra. Oakey's capital growth has averaged 15% a year over the past five years.

Infrastructure – good existing amenities and evidence of investment in major new projects

Sustainable growth locations have the core amenities that residents need: schools, shopping, public transport, medical services and sports and leisure facilities. But the game-changer can be investment in major new infrastructure. A big infrastructure project generates economic activity and employment in construction – often even more after completion than during – as well as improving the amenities or accessibility of the area. Roads, rail links, schools, universities, hospitals, airports – they all impact in different ways. In the 10 years before 2020, the Sunshine Coast was a tourist town with little capital growth. Then, a $20 billion program of infrastructure development transformed its economy and made it a national property market icon.

There will be more on this later, because it's a critical factor in outperformance.

Rental market – low vacancies likely to put upward pressure on rents

One of the hallmarks of a growth property market is low vacancies among rental properties. A vacancy rate below 2% indicates there is a high tenant demand and/or a shortage of supply. Rising rents and higher yields will attract investors and create competition for properties, putting upward pressure on prices. A vacancy rate of 4% or 5% indicates an oversupply of dwellings, perhaps caused by construction of too many new homes in the area – and a surplus of homes is the one factor that puts property prices into a downward spiral. It's noteworthy that in 2024 the cities with the lowest vacancy rates – Adelaide, Perth and Brisbane – were the leaders on price growth, while the cities with higher vacancy rates – Sydney and Melbourne – were experiencing little or no price growth.

Increasing employment opportunities – evidence of jobs growth locally

Many surveys over the years have revealed that a key factor dictating choice of location for buyers is proximity to where they work. Nobody wants to waste three hours of their day on the commute. Contrary to popular myth, most people do NOT work in the CBD. Most go to work in suburban employment nodes: shopping centres, industrial estates, universities, hospitals, data centres, suburban commercial precincts. In many of our cities, the biggest employment node is the airport and surrounding commercial-industrial zone. The Australian TradeCoast precinct, which is clustered around the airport and seaport in Brisbane, is that city's biggest centre of employment. The aerotropolis that will surround the new Western Sydney Airport will eventually be the biggest employment node in Greater Sydney. A major hospital typically employs 5000 or 6000 people. Wherever these employment zones are evolving, nearby suburbs will have property price growth.

Capital growth – strong sales activity pointing to future price rises

It gives comfort to buyers if their location of choice has a track record of good capital growth. But the past does not inform the future. There's no guarantee the growth leaders of the past five years will prevail in the next five. Underachievers in the past can become the national leaders when something changes in their economy. Perth had a decade of weak prices before becoming the national champion of price growth in 2023 and 2024. Ditto the Sunshine Coast before it shot to national fame in 2020 and beyond. Those changes in fortune occurred for identifiable reasons. At Hotspotting, we use key metrics to determine where locations sit in their local cycle and predict their future path – including sales volumes, which is one of the best forward indicators of future price changes.

Affordability – median house prices below a benchmark level

There's an outdated and discredited theory that the "better" suburbs show the highest price growth. The research has been disproving that notion for many years. Affordability rules in real estate. We might aspire to live in Toorak, Bondi Beach or Byron Bay, but most can't afford it. Aspiration doesn't create price growth: real demand does, and the great bulk of the demand goes to the affordable areas. In the five years after COVID, the top 10 locations for capital growth were all small regional centres with affordable house prices. In 2024 the leading jurisdictions for capital growth were the smaller cities and the regional markets, and the expensive capital cities of Sydney, Melbourne and Canberra were at the bottom of the pack. The price boom in Perth in 2023 and 2024 was led by the cheap areas; once the affordability factor evaporated through rampant price growth, the Perth boom faded. In Adelaide, the main challenger to Perth during that period, the highest price growth occurred in the cheapest markets in the northern suburbs. Halfway through 2025, the market leader on rising buyer and price growth was the cheapest capital city, Darwin.

Low risk – avoid volatile markets

The most volatile markets in Australia are the one-industry economies. They include mining towns, tourist resorts and small, rural communities. Any location sustained by one industry – whether it's the resources sector, tourism or agriculture – has a vulnerable property market, not only because they rely on a single industry sector but because those industries are volatile in nature. Mining is a boom-bust sector, tourism is vulnerable to bad weather and economic downturns, and agricultural economies can be decimated by drought or flood.

These markets can produce spurts of spectacular price growth, but they are not sustainable, and often the bust that follows a short, sharp boom can wipe out much of the previous gains. The median prices for iconic mining centres like Port Hedland in Western Australia and Moranbah in Queensland are lower today than they were more than a decade ago. Byron Bay, as discussed, recorded stunning price growth in the COVID boom period but has gone up and down like a roller coaster since. Anyone who hops on at the wrong time can lose a lot of money.

It's all about the economy

In February 2020, just before COVID-19 became part of the Australian reality, I wrote that regional Victoria was the nation's outstanding market. Multiple data sources supported the view that anyone seeking affordable property, good rental yields and great capital growth should consider regional Victoria. No other market jurisdiction in Australia had delivered so many locations with double-digit value growth in the previous 12 months. Regional Victoria was also a national leader in locations with strong long-term capital growth rates and featured prominently in CoreLogic's quarterly *Pain & Gain* report highlighting the number of properties sold for a profit in the September 2019 quarter.

Why was regional Victoria doing so well? Partly, it was because Victoria was ranked the number one economy in the nation and the number one state for population growth, gaining significantly from both overseas and internal migration. And Victoria's high ranking wasn't just about Melbourne – the regions had been major contributors to the state's success. Regional Victoria led the jurisdictions in jobs growth and had the lowest regional unemployment rate at 3.7%, the average regional rate being 5.1% at that time. In the previous five years, regional Victoria's unemployment rate had decreased by 2.9 percentage points. This theme of sturdy economic performance was also seen at a more local level, with regional centres such as Geelong, Bendigo and Ballarat delivering strong, diverse growth economies.

This was translating into exceptional performance in real estate. The *Pain & Gain* report, which compared the prices of properties sold in the September quarter with their previous sale, found that Hobart was the national leader – 98% of houses sold made a profit – but close behind in second place was regional Victoria, where 97% of houses sold for a price higher than the vendors paid previously (ahead of Melbourne's 96% and Sydney's 92%, and the national average of 90%).

The outperformance of locations in regional Victoria showed up in price-growth data for the previous year and also for the past decade. Dozens of locations had recorded double-digit growth in their median house prices over 12 months, while many had long-term capital growth rates above 7% per year, with some nudging 9% per year – which put them among the best in the nation.

These numbers illustrate three key points:

1. Economic performance translates into property performance.

2. Change is always happening in economies and real estate. Victoria's status as a strong economy eventually changed, particularly as it struggled more than most states to deal with the pandemic.

3. If the fundamentals are solid, recovery will eventually occur. In 2025 regional Victoria and Melbourne were seeing a real estate market revival.

Simon Pressley says, "The single biggest influence on any property market is always economic conditions". In the EMPIRICAL formula, the local economy is the pivotal factor. It's worth repeating this point: real estate is local in nature and real estate markets arise out of local economies. Hotspotting has location reports on all the LGA markets nationwide I rate as worthy of recommendation, and only five of the 20 pages of a typical report are devoted to the state of the current property market; the bulk of the report discusses the local economy, which will make or break the property market.

In the daily newsfeed service I subscribe to, in which my chosen keywords dictate which news articles I'm sent, the emphasis is on events that may change a local economy: infrastructure investment, project announcements, government policies and scraps of economic data that may cause a location to blip on my radar screen.

A report I value highly is the *State of the States* report published quarterly by CommSec. It analyses the state and territory economies based on eight key metrics. The formula is complex, but the outcome is simple and clear-cut: the eight states and territories are ranked from one to eight according to their overall economic strength. I'm interested in the correlation between those rankings and the strength of the capital-city property markets.

Here's how it looked in mid-2017. The CommSec rankings were as follows:

1. New South Wales
2. Victoria
3. Australian Capital Territory
4. Tasmania
5. South Australia
6. Queensland
7. Western Australia
8. Northern Territory

Here were my rankings of the capital-city property markets at that time, based on price growth:

1. Sydney
2. Melbourne
3. Canberra

4. Hobart
5. Adelaide
6. Brisbane
7. Perth
8. Darwin

The state economic rankings and the price performance of the capital cities aligned precisely. The two biggest cities were still rising strongly, Canberra was up moderately, Hobart was just starting to rise, Adelaide and Brisbane were lukewarm, and Perth and Darwin were falling. The correlation was too exact to be a coincidence.

Strong economies generate strong real estate demand. Jobs are being created, wages are strong, investment is happening, and things are being built. New residents are arriving to work on the new projects, consumers are spending, and confidence is high. From 2017 to 2019, Hobart and other markets in Tasmania rose. It would be overstating it to call it a boom – more of a mini-boom, less prolific than the earlier ones in Sydney and Melbourne – but there was significant price growth over two to three years in Hobart, Launceston and many of the smaller regional towns of Tasmania.

This followed the rise of the Tasmanian economy up the national pecking order. Traditionally, Tasmania had been something of an economic basket case, ranking last or second last on most economic parameters. However, after 2014 and a change of state government, proactive action, including increased infrastructure spending, helped to regenerate the Tasmanian economy.

By July 2019 it had risen to third among the states and territories in CommSec's *State of the States* report, and three months later it ranked second. This was an exceptional performance by an economic minnow. Out of that vibrant economic environment came a property up-cycle that extended throughout 2017, 2018 and 2019. And then, in April 2020, it was elevated to share the number one spot with Victoria. The media was slightly incredulous at the time. Tasmania was the leading economy in the nation? Seriously?

But all the data supported the idea. Tasmania, which had been a net loser on population in the past, was now achieving consistent growth. Unemployment, traditionally well above national averages, was now at low levels. The economy was growing and attracting investment. And consequently, throughout 2019 and 2020, property price data from a variety of sources regularly had Hobart as the leader among the capital cities.

PIPA research published in 2024 named the markets with the highest growth in house prices in the previous 20 years. Thanks largely to that extraordinary period of growth over the previous 10 years, regional Tasmania ranked number one in the nation and Hobart number three.

That correlation between state economies and market performance has been evident more recently as well. Throughout 2023 and 2024, the *State of the States* reports recorded a duel between South Australia and Western Australia for the number one ranking. Queensland was often next, mid-table were New South Wales and Tasmania, and the bottom-ranked economies were the Northern Territory, Victoria and the Australian Capital Territory. Throughout those two years, there was boom-level price growth in Adelaide and regional South Australia, Perth and regional Western Australia, and Brisbane and regional Queensland. Sydney and regional NSW had moderate price growth, and prices stagnated or fell in Melbourne, regional Victoria, Canberra, Hobart and Darwin. The four different types of markets – boom growth, moderate growth, no growth and falling prices – were all occurring somewhere, and they broadly aligned with the strength or weakness of the state or territory economy.

Early in 2025 the *State of the States* report recorded a significant improvement in the ranking of Victoria's economy, and we saw the first signs of recovery in the property markets of Melbourne and regional Victoria, which I recorded in the Winter 2025 edition of Hotspotting's *Price Predictor Index*.

Think LGAs rather than suburbs

Simon Pressley of Propertyology shares my view that real estate is local and that success depends on choosing the right locations to buy. He says high-quality property market intelligence about location is significantly more important than the bricks and mortar itself. That may startle many people, because most people put most focus on the property itself rather than where it sits.

But what is the key element of location? The media often runs features on "the best suburbs" for investment, and sometimes even "the best streets". It's great clickbait fodder, but it has little to do with the reality of realty. When it comes to pinpointing the places most likely to deliver outperformance, there's no evidence supporting the concept of a "best suburb" and a "best street". It might have some validity for the extreme upper end of the luxury market, which is all about prestige and image, but down in the mainstream, where most people live, those factors don't play a part.

Hotspotting was built around creating reports on LGAs, towns and regional centres. We don't write reports on individual suburbs; we write about clusters of suburbs. Usually, our reports focus on municipalities, or LGAs. A billion-dollar hospital constructed in Toowoomba doesn't just impact South Toowoomba, the suburb where it's being built, but the whole municipality of Toowoomba. The Moreton Bay Rail Link to the Redcliffe Peninsula in Brisbane's north (completed in 2016 after half a century of broken political promises) didn't just benefit Kippa-Ring, the suburb with the local station – it increased the prospects of all the suburbs on the peninsula and other suburbs along the route.

Simon Pressley has undertaken research allocating the degree of influence on capital growth by various core elements. He claims that only 20% of an individual property's capital growth can be attributed to the qualities of the property itself, 8% by the street and only 2% by the purchase price. The biggest impact, at 70%, comes from the city or town in which the property sits, not the suburb or the street:

> With far too many people, when they buy property, there's an unhealthy obsession with the bricks and mortar. They're thinking about the thing they can see and can touch. But none of these things are remotely relevant to property market performance. As a property investor, if you get the city selection wrong, it doesn't matter what piece of real estate you bought.

Employment nodes are pivotal

One of the enduring myths in real estate is the importance of proximity to the CBD. It's long been the greatest furphy, repeated often in news media.

There was a time – decades ago – when the CBD was key in our biggest cities. Most people worked there, a lot of the major shopping was there, and government services were concentrated there. Industrial property was often clustered close by.

Much is different in 21st-century Australia. Business has decentralised to cheaper suburban locations, suburban shopping centres (and online shopping) dominate retail, and government services are distributed across the metro area. Industrial property is out in the suburbs, close to key transport routes. Technology allowing more people to work remotely has further decentralised the workforce. The CBD is no longer the centre of a city's universe.

The media mostly continues to infer that most people work in the CBD. The reality is that most Australians work in suburban employment nodes: regional shopping centres; airports; hospitals; universities; commercial-industrial estates; massive data centres; huge distribution centres used by the big supermarkets and others. These are businesses that like to be located on major road networks – like the Gateway Motorway in Brisbane, the Metropolitan Ring Road in Melbourne and the Light Horse Interchange (the junction of the M4 and M7 motorways) in Western Sydney.

The trend away from the CBD has been underway for a long time. Ten years ago, research by the Committee for Sydney with consultancy PwC found that Sydney's economic centre was drifting away from the CBD towards Concord. *The Sydney Morning Herald* reported in April 2015, "The CBD is slowly becoming less important to Sydney. The city's economic centre of gravity – the point around which all economic output is evenly balanced – is at Concord, nine kilometres west of the CBD. And it has been drifting north-west for more than a decade". Similarly, Melbourne's economic centre of gravity was deemed to be 6.7km to the south of the CBD.

A decade later, the importance of CBDs has become increasingly diluted. Even without the work-from-home trend, it's apparent more and more people go to work in places other than the CBD.

There are massive employment nodes scattered across the Greater Sydney Area, such as Macquarie Park, Sydney Olympic Park and Parramatta. One of the biggest is the Eastern Creek precinct in Western Sydney. Businesses for which warehousing and logistics are important cluster there because of the motorway intersection – transport connectivity is key for these businesses. The CBD plays no part in their day-to-day activities. The importance of this precinct will grow when the new Western Sydney International Airport at Badgerys Creek is operational; the aerotropolis will make Western Sydney the biggest employment node in Australia. It's estimated there will be 200,000 people working there when all the infrastructure is in place, on the back of investment totalling tens of billions of dollars.

In Brisbane, the most important employment node is the Australia TradeCoast precinct. This is the cluster of commercial and industrial businesses that has evolved around Brisbane Airport and the Port of Brisbane, which are in close proximity. An estimated 110,000 people go to work there every day.

Education-medical precincts are among the most important of the suburban employment nodes – few things bring life to a community and a local property market than clusters of universities and hospitals. In Adelaide, the Flinders University main campus sits beside the Flinders Medical Centre and a number of other hospitals in a medical precinct. Not far away is the Tonsley Innovation District. In Sydney there are major education-medical precincts at Ryde, Westmead, Liverpool and elsewhere. In Melbourne the municipalities of Monash and Brimbank – and the inner-city precinct, including Parkville and Carlton – have university campuses and major hospitals in close proximity. Perth has major nodes based on hospitals and education campuses at Murdoch and Joondalup, among others. In Logan City in Brisbane's south, Griffith University and Logan Hospital are in close proximity. These facilities generate economic activity, provide employment and supply essential services. Those who work or study there want to live nearby if possible.

For the workers employed in those businesses, the CBD is irrelevant. They don't work there, they don't shop there, they don't access services there and their kids don't go to school there. They have no reason to ever visit the CBD. Maybe they'll go to a show or access some other entertainment in the city every once in a while, but when it comes to choosing a place to buy a home, they're more likely to be thinking of suburbs with good access to one of these employment nodes.

And if you cling to the cliché that outer-ring locations don't show good capital growth, have a look at some of the long-term growth rates (average annual growth in prices over five years) in these suburbs in Sydney in mid-2025:

- Blacktown, 8.7%
- Seven Hills, 10%
- Rooty Hill, 10.1%
- Colyton, 9.4%
- Campbelltown, 10%
- Macquarie Fields, 9.4%

At these growth rates, real estate is doubling in value in seven or eight years. Compare that to suburbs in the Inner West, close the Sydney CBD:

- Balmain, 6.3%
- Newtown, 5.8%
- Ashfield, 6.5%
- Petersham, 6.7%
- Rozelle, 4.7%

Chapter 9

New trends

Recently, there has been commentary about apartments challenging houses on capital growth potential. The evidence against this is, at face value, compelling. Houses have consistently outperformed units on value growth since records were first kept, so why would anyone invest in attached dwellings when detached houses are so demonstrably superior?

This argument falls down on one key element: it precludes the possibility of change.

My observation after 40-plus years as a researcher-writer on Australian real estate is that change is constantly happening. It's what makes my job so stimulating. If I can encapsulate the mission of my Hotspotting business in a single short phrase, it's to identify and understand change. Sniffing out game-changing new things before everyone knows about them is the secret sauce at the real estate banquet.

One of my favourite sayings is this: the past does not inform the future. One of Australia's smartest analysts, Simon Pressley of Propertyology, observed that the busiest markets in three years' time are probably flat today. Equally, the national leaders today won't be next year. For decades, the dominant demographic force was the population drift to the big cities; now, there's an exodus in the opposite direction. Stigmatised suburbs have become trendy through gentrification. Periods in which Sydney and Melbourne have dominated capital growth have been superseded by eras in which the smaller cities have led the nation. Since COVID the best performers have all been regional centres.

And now the most dominant of all real estate paradigms – that houses always top units on value growth – is undergoing a notable challenge.

The essence of success in real estate is to be among the first to see change coming, because that's where the big growth is.

The rise and rise of apartments

In the 40-plus years I've been researching and writing about housing markets, the dominant paradigm of real estate has been that houses outperform units on price growth. Attached dwellings – units, townhouses and apartments – had inferior growth because they lacked land content, according to conventional wisdom.

In June 2025 Hotspotting and investment advisory Nuestar published the report *The New Paradigm in Real Estate: The Rise and Rise of Apartments* analysing price growth in Australian capital cities in the 12 months to May 2025. In half of the markets in Sydney, Brisbane, Perth, Adelaide and Hobart, apartments outperformed houses. Brisbane was the trend leader, with apartments recording higher value growth than houses in 76% of locations. Close behind was Perth at 75% and Sydney at 71%. The report was featured in news media across Australia. I was happy to see the publicity but bemused that so many journalists saw it as news, because we'd been shouting about this trend for a number of years. Houses versus apartments has been a regular debate over the years, but it's taken time for the challenge of apartments to be broadly recognised.

The *PIPA Annual Investor Sentiment Survey 2020* found 74% of investors preferred standalone houses, with only 5% opting for apartments and 6% townhouses. (The remaining 15% selected other options or had no preference.) That was unsurprising – real estate 101 has always stated that houses outperform units on capital growth. It's the land content issue – many will quote the beloved property cliché that land appreciates and buildings depreciate.

Like so much in real estate commentary, it's a generalisation. There are many counters to that argument. Many people don't want land content because it means lawnmowing and weeding; they prefer a low-maintenance, lock-up-and-leave type of lifestyle. And the land content keeps getting smaller – the quarter-acre (1000-square-metre) block is a museum piece, replaced by 400- or 300-square-metre strips of dirt, most of it consumed by the footprint of the house. Houses in modern estates are so close to their neighbours they're little different to a townhouse.

A 2023 study by Infrastructure Victoria found that the typical apartment was superior than houses on suburban blocks in terms of location, being closer to public transport, shops, services and amenities. And they're usually much cheaper. There's also the possibility of a commanding view from an apartment, something most houses don't have.

A new factor that has emerged in recent years is safety and security. In our biggest cities in particular, there is growing concern about crime, notably burglaries, home invasions and car theft. More and more people feel threatened at street level and more secure in an apartment building with security features and off-street parking.

So, now in Australia we have a variety of cohorts for whom attached dwellings are more desirable than detached houses on land:

- downsizers vacating the four-bedroom family home and seeking something smaller and easier to maintain
- lifestyle-seekers who like the low-maintenance, lock-up-and-leave aspect
- migrants from countries where attached dwellings are the norm
- buyers seeking proximity to key features without the huge price tag
- young buyers seeking an affordable entry into the market.

I looked at this situation in an online column in October 2019. I noted that apartment markets were leading Melbourne's recovery from its post-boom downturn. Hotspotting's spring survey that year identified 73 markets where median prices had risen in the past 12 months, and 79% of them were apartment markets, including:

- Fairfield (up 20%)
- Glen Huntly (up 15%)
- Niddrie (up 15%)
- Toorak (up 17%)
- West Footscray (up 15%)
- Yarraville (up 15%).

The most striking trend was the number of suburbs where the median house price was down but the median apartment price was up. This scenario appeared in 53 suburbs across Greater Melbourne, including:

- Brighton (houses down 18% but units up 8%)
- Doncaster East (houses down 13% but units up 9%)
- Heidelberg (houses down 13% but units up 11%)
- Highett (houses down 20% but units up 9%)
- Kensington (houses down 14% but units up 8%)
- Mount Waverley (houses down 14% but units up 6%)
- Ormond (houses down 16% but units up 13%)
- West Footscray (houses down 10% but units up 15%).

Melbourne's most expensive market, Toorak, provided the starkest contrast: the median house price had dropped 29% to $3.1 million in the past year, while the median apartment price had risen 17% to $985,000. In addition to the contrast in growth performance, the standout feature was the big price difference, a key attraction for those who favour attached dwellings.

There were 48 markets where the median price was down in annual terms but had risen in the latest quarter – and two-thirds of those were apartment markets. In addition, there were 129 markets where median prices were down 10% or more in annual terms – 110 of them were house markets and only 19 were unit markets.

That Melbourne situation was an outlier in 2019 – in most places, houses still ruled. But that's no longer the case. The afore-mentioned Hotspotting and Nuestar report *The New Paradigm in Real Estate* observed that apartments had recorded higher or at least equal median price growth than houses in 63% of Australia's capital-city LGAs. There were seven markets where apartments led houses in growth in the past 12 months by 20 percentage points or above. East Brisbane led the pack with a 32% difference – its median house price ($1.411 million) dropped 7% in the past 12 months, while its median apartment price ($670,000) increased by 25%. Again, the price differential is a key factor, with apartments less than half the price of houses.

In Perth, rising house prices meant more buyers were turning to its more affordable apartment market, with 75% of suburbs analysed recording higher apartment price growth than house price growth in the previous 12 months. The best performer was Lathlain, where the median apartment price ($475,000) grew by 26% in the previous 12 months while the median house price ($982,000) dropped by 1%.

In Sydney, 71% of apartment markets outperformed house markets. The best performers were in the more expensive suburbs, where apartments offered buyers an opportunity to enjoy all the same amenities and outlooks that those living in more expensive houses enjoy but for a fraction of the price. Little Bay had the biggest difference in growth in the previous 12 months at 39%, with its median apartment price ($1.36 million) up by 40% and its median house price ($2.77 million) up by just 1%.

The data showed the push towards apartment living was helping drive up prices in many near-city locations at a faster pace than house markets. The report said, "Australians of all ages are embracing something owners and investors in big cities around the world have done for decades – a more affordable and low-maintenance lifestyle that comes with apartment living".

Simon Pressley of Propertyology published an infographic in May 2025 showing that in the decade to the end of 2024, detached dwellings outgrew attached dwellings in every capital city. In Sydney, houses rose 93% and units 29%. In Melbourne it was 59% versus 27%, and in Canberra 79% versus 43%. It was a lot closer in Hobart (96% versus 91%) and Adelaide (93% versus 75%), but the figures confirmed the historic supremacy of houses on capital growth. Others, including InvestorKit and CoreLogic, published figures in mid-2025 showing that historic dominance of houses on capital growth. However, I believe those days are over. There has been a dramatic paradigm shift in the past two years, and increasingly units are overtaking houses on price growth. CoreLogic research published in 2025 found that in the previous 12 months units had shown higher price growth than houses in 60% of suburbs nationwide and in 87% of suburbs in Brisbane. Research published by PropTrack in mid-2025 found that nationally and in Melbourne, Brisbane, Adelaide and Perth, unit-price growth had been higher than house-price growth over the previous 12 months. The trend extended to regional areas too, with unit prices up 5.3% compared to 4.5% for houses.

It should be noted that the trend is not universal, but there is a growing number of areas where apartments are outdoing houses. For investors, this is a milestone event. Units have long been cheaper and had better rental yields, particularly if you avoided the high-rise buildings with lifts and lots of amenities (and therefore high body corporate fees), but the lack of comparable capital growth was a problem; however, with attached dwellings now competing with houses on value growth, they become a win-win-win situation for investors.

The exodus to affordable lifestyle

Game-changing trends are among the most powerful drivers of outperformance in real estate. Perhaps the most significant in the 21st century is the exodus to affordable lifestyle.

Australia is strongly tilted towards the capital cities. That's where most Australians live and where the greatest share of property sales take place. Over 60% of the population lives in the five biggest cities, and there is copious media commentary telling us that the best and safest investments are in the big cities. Like much of what media offers, this is misleading.

Throughout most of the past 100 years in Australia, population has been drifting from the country to the cities. However, the exodus to affordable lifestyle has become one of the most compelling trends in Australian real estate and has had a dramatic impact on price growth.

The *PIPA Annual Investor Sentiment Survey 2020* found that 61% of investors favoured capital cities for investment, while only 34% would buy in regional or coastal locations. And yet, the highest price growth in the next five years occurred, overwhelmingly, in regional centres, with the best of the capital cities well down the list of best achievers.

Much has changed since 2020. Propertyology research has revealed that of the 137 municipalities in the eight capital cities, 89 have experienced falling populations due to internal migration – people leaving the city and heading for the regions. Those who have left the cities to move to the country areas in the past 10 years outnumber the population of the Gold Coast, our sixth biggest city.

Simon Pressley of Propertyology was among the first to recognise the significance of the trend. He noted in a 2020 analysis that there were different categories of people relocating from the big cities. Some, he said, had brought forward their retirement, and were selling the four-bedroom family home in the big city and buying a comparable home in a more affordable place in a regional area, creating a reserve of cash by moving house. Others were working from home and realised they didn't need to be in the city anymore. The trend gained further momentum when the COVID lockdowns prompted more big-city dwellers to abscond, notably from Melbourne, where Victorian Premier Daniel Andrews turned the city into the most locked-down place on the planet.

In 2020, Pressley said:

People have been leaving the bigger, expensive cities for quite some time. Sydney loses 20,000 to 25,000 net every year. Melbourne previously was gaining through internal migration but last financial year – the year to June 2019 – it gained only 590 people. For a population of 5 million people, that doesn't even register. The only two capital cities that gained population from internal migration were Brisbane and Hobart – but Brisbane gained only 0.6%. That's pre-COVID. The next set of figures will show an even bigger surge towards the regions. And they will also be pre-COVID. And then the next batch will be off the charts.

Recently, he said:

Claiming that the biggest cities provide the best growth is as intelligent as saying it only rains on the days that the rubbish is collected. Seventeen of the 20 most expensive locations in Australia are not capital cities – many of them have a population of less than 50,000. Claiming that the cities have always outperformed the regions is stupidity on steroids: 53 regional townships have had a higher capital growth rate over the past 10 years than the best-performed capital city.

Early in 2025 CoreLogic published its list of cities and towns with the highest percentage growth in house prices in the previous five years – since COVID arrived early in 2020. The top 10 locations on the list, and 18 of the top 20, were regional centres. The best performing capital city, Perth, ranked 14th, while Adelaide was in 16th place. Many of the leading performers were places many Australians would know little about if they'd heard of them at all.

The top 10 are listed in the next chapter. The common features: they're all small, affordable regional centres.

The top three, even after five years of stellar price growth, still had median house prices below $500,000. Murray Bridge – on the Murray River, a little beyond the Adelaide Hills – recorded a 101% rise in its median house price in five years, effectively doubling to $496,000. Kingaroy, the key town in the South Burnett region in southern Queensland, rose 96% to $468,000. Geraldton, the largest Western Australian population centre north of Perth, increased 94% in five years to $494,000.

The price rises in these rural areas occurred through a combination of new residents arriving (as part of the "exodus to affordable lifestyle" trend) and investors chasing affordability and higher rental yields.

For investors, buying in a good regional city is a win-win-win situation, with more affordable prices, higher rental yields and great prospects for capital growth – if you choose the right location. Not every country town is going to deliver; it needs to have a strong and diverse local economy with infrastructure investment in the mix.

For home buyers, these locations offer a different and more affordable lifestyle, leaving behind the negative aspects of life in the big, expensive, congested cities. They've been moving from Sydney and Melbourne in significant numbers for over a decade, contrary to media misreporting of the trend as a COVID-inspired phenomenon, and the trend has continued strongly since the lockdowns ended.

The research has verified this trend for many years. The price data showed that, in the five years to 2020, key regional cities in New South Wales outperformed Sydney on capital growth, the best of regional Victoria had higher price growth than Melbourne, regional areas in Queensland such as the Sunshine Coast did considerably better than Brisbane, and multiple regional centres in South Australia had much higher price growth than Adelaide.

The Winter 2019 edition of Hotspotting's *Price Predictor Index*, which analyses sales activity as a precursor to price growth, also demonstrated that the regions were outperforming the capital cities. That report depicted very strong performance by regional Australia generally and explained why so many of the nation's growth markets were found in the regions – places like Ballarat, Bendigo, Wagga Wagga, Orange, Ballina, Port Stephens, Mackay, Rockhampton, Toowoomba and the Sunshine Coast.

Individual locations in regional areas dominated in the *National Top 50 List of Supercharged Suburbs* report (which lists the suburbs and towns with the strongest rises in buyer activity), part of the Winter 2019 *Price Predictor Index*. Thirty of the featured locations were in regional areas and only 20 were in capital cities. Most of these locations would excel on price growth over the next three to five years. Some of them, like Rockhampton, would be among the most frenzied markets in the nation, with multiple buyers competing for every home for sale, pushing up prices rapidly.

At that time, regional New South Wales was not following Sydney's negative trend. While most sectors of the Sydney market were in decline in 2019, the cities and towns of regional New South Wales had been delivering many growth markets for two years. I wrote in the Winter 2019 edition of the *Price Predictor Index*, "In many cases there's a lot more real estate growth going on than anyone realises. Nine out of ten locations in Tasmania have median prices higher than last year. It's similar for 60% of regional New South Wales, 61% of regional Queensland and 80% of regional Victoria".

In 2025 there continues to be strong performance in regional areas. While the media has focused in recent years on the boom results in Perth, Adelaide and Brisbane, the regional areas of Western Australia, South Australia and Queensland have delivered outstanding growth without attracting a lot of attention.

Regional South Australia is the unsung hero of Australian real estate. It's never included in the conversation about the best places to buy, but it has been a stellar performer. That list of top growth markets since COVID had Murray Bridge as number one in the nation, but also prominent in the national rankings were Victor Harbor, Mount Gambier, Port Lincoln and Port Pirie.

Chapter 10

The areas to watch

Real estate consumers often fixate on the idea that individual suburbs will do better than their neighbours. I'm often asked for my opinion of one suburb or another on the basis that the target location has special qualities and will outperform others. Often the qualities a consumer lists about a suburb they like have existed for 50 or more years, which begs the question: why will those features cause the suburb to outperform this year or next?

The reality is that it's rare for one suburb to star while its neighbours underperform. Market performance tends to happen in clusters, with a group of suburbs being influenced by the same factors, such as a major new piece of infrastructure.

How my 2019 nominations panned out

In August 2019 I published my list of the top 10 municipalities nationwide in terms of growth momentum based on analysis of sales activity. This was a milestone list in terms of outcomes in both the short and longer term. Seven of the 10 LGAs were in Perth, Brisbane and Adelaide, which went on to be the national price-growth leaders over the following five years. Another was the Sunshine Coast, which was a national leader in price growth between 2020 and 2023 (and showing signs of beginning another growth spurt in 2025). Another was Bendigo, which became a notable performer in the regional Victoria market.

Here are those LGAs or suburban clusters, what I wrote about them in 2019 and how they performed over the next five years.

Brisbane North, Qld

In 2019 I wrote:

> The Brisbane North precinct (the northern suburbs of the Brisbane City Council area, which benefit from the Gateway Motorway, rail links and proximity to both Brisbane Airport and the Port of Brisbane) is the most active part of the Brisbane market, which is poised for stronger growth. This middle-ring area has 10 suburbs with rising sales demand, including Alderley, where quarterly sales have been 28, 37, 48 and 50 in the past year: its median prices have risen 5% for houses and 22% for units. The other growth suburbs are Boondall, Chermside West, Everton Park, Kedron, McDowall, Sandgate, Stafford, Stafford Heights and Wavell Heights. These are all middle-market areas with median prices in the $600,000s and $700,000s.

Since then, the median house price for Alderley has risen from around $770,000 to $1.5 million. Most suburbs in this precinct of Brisbane have recorded capital growth averaging around 12% per year, which means values doubling in six years. All those locations with median house prices in the $600,000s and $700,000s are now well north of $1 million.

Sunshine Coast, Qld

In 2019 I wrote:

The Sunshine Coast, boosted by a massive program of infrastructure investment, continues to be the strongest of the Queensland markets, both in terms of rising sales activity and price growth. It's rising while the more high-profile Gold Coast market is falling. The Sunshine Coast has 10 suburbs with rising buyer demand and another 13 have consistent sales activity. Landsborough and Little Mountain feature on our *National Top 50* list. Over 60% of regional Queensland markets have median prices higher than a year ago. Of these, 21 have increased by more than 10%, and 10 of those 21 locations are Sunshine Coast suburbs, led by Eumundi (28%), Sunshine Beach (15%), Twin Waters (15%) and Wurtulla (15%).

Since then, the "exodus to affordable lifestyle" trend has raised the status of the Sunshine Coast, which has ranked as the number one destination nationwide for internal migrants within Australia. The investment in infrastructure has continued, with the region's airport now international and a new CBD evolving at Maroochydore. Most Sunshine Coast suburbs have recorded growth in house values averaging at least 12% a year over the past five years, with some as high as 15% per year (values have doubled in five years). Apartment markets have had similar growth rates.

Charles Sturt, SA

In 2019 I wrote:

The Charles Sturt LGA extends north-west from central Adelaide out to the beaches and includes a range of good suburbs, including eight where sales activity is rising steadily. They include inner-city Brompton (where quarterly sales have been 23, 32, 38 and 50) as well as middle-market suburbs like Findon, Seaton, Flinders Park (quarterly sales 22, 25, 25, 32, 35 and 38), Woodville South and Fulham Gardens. Henley Beach and West Beach also have growth momentum. Good price growth is happening in this area, including Henley Beach South (median house price up 15% to $985,000).

All the suburbs of the Charles Sturt LGA have seen values rise at double-digit growth rates in the five years since, with most averaging between 11% and 15% per year. In mid-2025 Henley Beach and Henley Beach South both had median house prices above $1.6 million.

Marion, SA

In 2019 I wrote:

The Marion LGA – a middle-market area in the south-west of Adelaide boosted by major medical, education and innovation campuses – has been a market leader for the past 18 months and is once again a standout market. It has nine suburbs with rising sales patterns, including Ascot Park, Edwardstown, Glengowrie, Hallett Cove, Marion, O'Halloran Hill and Seacombe Gardens. Warradale makes our *National Top 50* list of rising suburbs: its median house price of $595,000 is typical of the Marion LGA's middle-ring affordability.

Adelaide has been the nation's most consistently strong market in the five years since, with values rising and rising. It was the main challenger to Perth's status as the national leader on price growth in 2024. The Marion LGA has been a consistent performer: every suburb has averaged at least 10% per year growth in house values over five years, and most have achieved between 12% and 14%. The best, Seacliff Park, has averaged 15% per year, rising from $520,000 to $1.11 million.

Port Adelaide Enfield, SA

In 2019 I wrote:

> The Port Adelaide Enfield LGA emerged in 2018 as an up-and-coming market in the SA capital – and continues to be one of the busiest precincts in Adelaide. Our latest survey reveals seven suburbs with rising activity, including Croydon Park, Dernancourt, Greenacres, North Haven, Rosewater and Royal Park. Dernancourt features in our *National Top 50* list. This precinct is being boosted by major local events, including the massive program of building vessels for the Australian Navy and ongoing development around the port. The Osborne Naval Shipyard is undergoing a $535 million upgrade to accommodate the building of 40 new Defence craft, 500 public servants are being moved here, and a new rail spur is proposed to link the port's commercial centre and the Dock One residential precinct to the Adelaide CBD.

Since then, the evolution of Port Adelaide Enfield as a leading residential precinct between the Adelaide CBD and the port has continued, helped by that multi-billion-dollar shipbuilding enterprise. In five years, Birkenhead's median house price has lifted from $415,000 to $836,000, North Haven's from $460,000 to $900,000 and Semaphore's from $660,000 to $1.2 million. Most suburbs in this LGA have performed similarly.

Onkaparinga, SA

In 2019 I wrote:

As we have observed many times, Onkaparinga always features prominently in our analysis of the Adelaide market. It currently has seven suburbs with growth momentum – including Aldinga Beach (where quarterly sales have been 54, 63, 67 and 70), which features in our *National Top 50 List of Supercharged Suburbs*. Other growth markets include Christies Beach, Hackham, Happy Valley, Old Reynella and Seaford. This LGA ticks a lot of boxes for investors: it has lifestyle, affordability, improved transport links, economic growth drivers, population growth and proximity to major jobs nodes.

Since then, upgrades to transport links, both rail and motorway, have been a game-changer for this lifestyle market with beaches and a renowned wine district in Adelaide's south. It prospered due to a magic potion of affordable prices, lifestyle features and transport infrastructure investment. Long-term capital growth rates around 10% to 12% per year are common in Adelaide, but this LGA is on another level. Many suburbs have recorded between 16% and 19% per year. Hackham West has averaged 21% per year, which means its median price doubled in less than four years. Many Onkaparinga suburbs remain relatively affordable, with median house prices in the $600,000s and $700,000s.

Joondalup, WA

In 2019 I wrote:

The Joondalup LGA continues to be a standout for its steadiness and resilience against the Perth downturn and is poised to lead the city's market recovery. It now has eight suburbs with rising sales momentum, which makes it number one in Perth and among the best of the nation's LGAs. The suburbs of this LGA are based around the Joondalup CBD, which is a centre for infrastructure and services for Perth's north. Growth markets include Burns Beach, Duncraig, Edgewater, Greenwood, Joondalup, Mullaloo and Padbury, many of which offer good affordability.

Back then I was writing about the prolonged market downturn in Perth but suggesting that a recovery was looming. I continued to predict an up-cycle for the Perth market, and it became the national leader on price growth for three years, underpinned by a nation-leading state economy, significant infrastructure investment and major population growth. Joondalup, which has a suburban CBD of key education, medical, transport and retail facilities, thrived amid Perth's boom. Duncraig's median house value went from $750,000 to $1.27 million in four years, Padbury's from $670,000 to $990,000 in two years and Craigie's from $570,000 to $810,000 in two years.

Melville, WA

In 2019 I wrote:

The City of Melville in Perth's inner south is one of the precincts leading the market fightback in the WA capital. It has seven growth markets and seven consistent performers. Suburbs with rising sales demand include Attadale, Bull Creek, Kardinya, Leeming, Mt Pleasant and Palmyra – some of which are million-dollar suburbs but most of which are middle-market areas. The star is Willagee, which makes our *National Top 50* list with quarterly sales of 25,

39, 46 and 51 – and the latest quarter also shows sign of growth in the median house price ($520,000).

Certain types of market are consistently solid performers. The Melville LGA is one of them. It has good proximity to desirable features (the Fremantle port precinct, the Swan River, the Perth CBD), important infrastructure (Murdoch University and Fiona Stanley Hospital), good services and amenities (schools, shops, lots of green space, the river) and plenty of nice real estate but without outrageous prices. It's a place with good real estate bones (that is, all the basic elements of what many people desire in a location). It's notable that Melville was resistant to the prolonged Perth downturn after the resources investment boom ended, it was a leader of the city's market revival, it did as well as anywhere during the 2020s boom and it was resilient as the boom was fading in 2025. And Willagee, mentioned in my report in 2019, rose from $520,000 to almost $1 million in 2025. Riverside Bicton went from $775,000 to $1.53 million in five years.

Belconnen, ACT

In 2019 I wrote:

> I regard Canberra as the strongest real estate economy in Australia, with the nation's highest average incomes and the lowest unemployment. It is challenging Victoria for the number one ranking on population growth, it has low vacancies and it often leads on rental growth. The Belconnen district is Canberra's number one jurisdiction for suburbs with rising sales activity. This precinct has a number of affordable suburbs, vacancies are well below 1%, rental yields are solid and some suburbs have grown their median prices 6% to 7% in the past 12 months.

It's interesting to read my analysis then because much has changed. In 2019 the Australian Capital Territory was at the top of its game, with a strongly ranked economy, low unemployment and high population growth. It led the nation on price growth in 2020. It has deteriorated since then, and in the April 2025 edition of *State of the States* its economy was ranked seventh out of the eight states and territories. Its population growth was well below the national average, and there was a notable absence of infrastructure projects. The ALP has ruled for over 20 years but relies on the support of the Greens – a situation almost guaranteed to create stagnation and real estate atrophy, given the Greens' advocacy of policies that discourage real estate development and investment.

Bendigo, Vic.

In 2019 I wrote:

> Bendigo is now the leading market in Victoria in terms of the number of suburbs with rising demand, having overtaken other strong markets like Geelong and Ballarat. It's attracting both home buyers and investors out of Melbourne chasing affordability and/or better rental yields in a growth centre. Many Bendigo suburbs have median prices in the $300,000s, emphasising the city's affordability. Bendigo is rising because of its own inherent strengths – including a strong and diverse economy, boosted by infrastructure spending – and its strong links to Melbourne.

Bendigo experienced major growth in property values over the three years that followed, flatlined for two years and then started to rise again as a classic second-wind market. Over three years from June 2020 to June 2023, Eaglehawk's median house price rose from $339,000 to $525,000; in little more than two years, Flora Hill went from $380,000 to $560,000. After a two-year market pause, they and other Bendigo suburbs were rebounding in 2025. The revival coincided with improvement in the ranking of the Victorian economy and population growth boosted by Melbourne residents escaping the big city as part of the "exodus to affordable lifestyle" trend.

Case studies: the nation's top 10 for price growth

The list of leading capital growth locations would puzzle most people. Why all these places we've never heard of and not Byron Bay, the Gold Coast or Noosa? The answer is that while most people think real estate growth is about glitz and glamour, it's sweat and muscle that matter most. The common features of most of the outperformers are strong economies, infrastructure investment, lifestyle factors and affordable prices.

Early in 2025 CoreLogic published its list of cities and towns with the highest percentage growth in house prices in the previous five years. Here are the top 10:

1. Murray Bridge, SA (101%)
2. Kingaroy, Qld (96%)
3. Geraldton, WA (94%)
4. Gympie, Qld (94%)
5. Busselton, WA (93%)
6. Bundaberg, Qld (93%)
7. Warwick, Qld (90%)
8. Maryborough, Qld (89%)
9. Hervey Bay, Qld (85%)
10. Gladstone, Qld (84%)

One of the fun facts hidden within this list is how resilient property markets are in defiance of natural disasters. Gympie and Maryborough have experienced many floods, for example, but their property prices continue to excel.

1. Murray Bridge

In mid-2020, the average house in this small regional centre in South Australia sold for around $230,000. Five years later the median price was approaching $500,000. How could real estate double in value in this unheralded town in five years and lead the nation in price growth?

My *Hotspots* reports alerted buyers to its potential in 2022, when it was included in a national report about affordable places with growth potential. South Australia was rising up the rankings of the state and territory economies, impacting real estate not only in Adelaide but also in regional centres not far from the capital. Murray Bridge offered plenty: a location on the Murray River not far from the prestigious suburbs of the Adelaide Hills but considerably more affordable, a multi-faceted economy, and lifestyle advantages that have made it an aquatic playground for Adelaide. There has been extensive investment in businesses, and the region has attracted a $7.5 billion proposal to create the Gifford Hill satellite city development for over 40,000 residents.

2. Kingaroy

Until Kingaroy became recognised as a price-growth leader recently, its main claim to notoriety was that Joh Bjelke-Peterson, Premier of Queensland for almost 20 years, was a peanut farmer in the region. Kingaroy remains Australia's leading peanut producer, and it also has the nation's largest pork processing plant, with the annual Kingaroy BaconFest a major event.

Apart from its extensive agricultural economy, though, Kingaroy has a significant tourism industry, is a noted wine district and is a major energy generator – several billion-dollar alternative energy developments are set to replace the ageing coal-fired power stations in the area. There's a lot going on in this local economy, and when that is combined with affordable housing – the median price was around $250,000 in 2020 – new residents are attracted. That brings new investment, including recently a $130 million private hospital and a sprawling Bunnings warehouse complex.

3. Geraldton

Western Australia was ranked among the top two state and territory economies in 2023, 2024 and 2025. That pumped up real estate markets not only in Perth but throughout the state. As the largest population centre north of Perth, with a key export port and major links to the resources sector, Geraldton was well situated to catch the growth wave. Government investment was impacting the region, including expansion of the port.

As a seaside centre about four hours north of the state capital, Geraldton had all the key elements of the growth formula: a growth economy, infrastructure investment, lifestyle benefits and affordable housing. It has often featured in the *Hotspots* reports published by my business and will continue to appear as a regional city with long-term growth credentials.

4. Gympie

Gympie is the poster boy for the downtrodden and stigmatised towns and suburbs of Australia, sometimes characterised as a crime-ridden "hell town". However, having studied this town in depth, I know there's a lot more to Gympie that most realise.

It's one of the price-growth leaders of Australia despite being clustered around a river that floods rather too often. It's a little north of Noosa and is a total contrast to the trendy seaside enclave. Gympie has a vibrant economy, and it has good road and rail links to Brisbane and is connected to the Sunshine Coast via an upgraded motorway. Infrastructure spending has boosted local employment, including billions of dollars spent upgrading the Bruce Highway south, north and around the town. There are also big alternative energy developments in the area.

The median house price has gone from $275,000 to $575,000 in little more than five years, while new development suburb Southside has doubled to almost $700,000 in the same period. It's not often thought of as a lifestyle town, but Gympie has the Mary River, a gorgeous coastline nearby and postcard countryside all around it.

5. Busselton

With the economy of Western Australia consistently among the nation's best, and with the state leading on population growth, there have been flow-on impacts to the key regional markets south of Perth, including Mandurah, Bunbury and Busselton. The Busselton region thrives on lifestyle and tourism, with its beautiful beaches and protected bays, and its status as the gateway to the Margaret River region, and road upgrades further north around Bunbury have made it easier to get there.

It has attracted steady buyer demand since 2021, and there was a jump in buyer numbers early in 2025. In 2020 you could buy houses in Dunsborough in the low $600,000s but by the end of 2024 the median house price was $1.2 million. In West Busselton, the median house price rose from $430,000 in mid-2020 to $820,000 five years later. This region doesn't have the economic diversity I prefer but has thrived on its lifestyle offering as part of the "exodus to affordable lifestyle" trend.

6. Bundaberg

Some places ooze prosperity, and Bundaberg, with rich, fertile soil and manicured downtown areas, is one such place. It's where most of Australia's sweet potatoes and macadamia nuts are grown and the legendary Bundaberg Rum is brewed. It has an airport and an export port, a tourism industry – which includes the Mon Repos Turtle Centre and the city's big river – manufacturing businesses and a major impending impetus from a $1.2 billion hospital project. As I write this, Bundaberg is a second-wind market – it sprinted from 2020 to 2022 inclusive, paused to catch its breath for a couple of years and was starting to run again in 2025. The hospital project will be a game-changer, both during construction and once operational, bringing thousands of new residents to the city – so that growth spurt from 2020 to 2025 is likely to be repeated.

7. Warwick

I'm willing to wager that 90% of readers are saying, "Where?" I was a tad surprised by this one myself, even though we included Warwick in some of our *Hotspots* reports in 2022 and 2023 because it was a prosperous agricultural town, had a couple of big energy projects in planning (including the $2 billion MacIntyre Wind Farm, Australia's largest) and was a cheaper alternative to booming Toowoomba up the road. And of course, the $31 billion Inland Rail link is coming its way. If you paid around $250,000 for the typical Warwick house in 2020, you'd be over $200,000 richer today. The vacancy rate in 2025 was 0.6%, so you wouldn't have any trouble finding a tenant, either.

8. Maryborough

Maryborough, like Gympie, was built alongside the Mary River and has a similar history of floods – and, like Gympie, Maryborough has defied those natural disasters to make the national top 10 for price growth.

Maryborough is part of the Fraser Coast region but is inland and more of a working town. Its industries include Downer Rail, which builds trains for Queensland Rail, and Maryborough Sugar Factory. Agriculture and timber are important industries, as is tourism – and Maryborough markets itself as the "Heritage City of Queensland". Despite two major floods in 2022, the town's median house price has risen steadily from 2020 to 2025 – from $210,000 to $450,000.

Maryborough has thrived on that magic formula: lifestyle features, affordable housing and a diverse economy creating jobs. And an unpredictable river has not been able to drown its growth potential.

9. Hervey Bay

Hervey Bay is a best-practice case study for the "exodus to affordable lifestyle" trend. This location has been referred to as "sea change for battlers" and has attracted retirees, first-home buyers and investors because it provides a relaxed coastal lifestyle without the tourist hordes, high-rises and expense of the Gold Coast.

Part of the Fraser Coast region (like Maryborough), it has great waters for fishing and whale watching, sheltered by the world-renowned K'gari (Fraser Island). Previously a tad vulnerable economically because of a reliance on tourism, the local economy has strengthened and diversified through investment in major projects across the commercial, industrial, renewable energy, health and transport sectors. Its population is projected to rise from 55,000 to close to 100,000 by 2041. Around the time COVID struck, the typical house in seaside Torquay cost around $320,000, and five years later it's $670,000. So, like others on this elite list, Hervey Bay has risen by offering lifestyle at an affordable price, underpinned by an expanding economy.

10. Gladstone

In 2010 and 2011 Gladstone was the market every investor wanted to be in: $60 billion was being invested in LNG processing plants and everyone assumed massive demand for housing. Developers built feverishly and investors grabbed anything they could – and by the time they realised the workforce was being accommodated in temporary camps they had created a market-busting housing glut. Vacancies went above 10% and rents, instead of going through the roof, fell through the floor. Prices followed. It took a decade for the oversupply to be absorbed and property values to get back to 2010 levels.

Gladstone is a different place today. It's no longer a goldrush town; it's a strong and stable regional centre with a growing population, an important export port and investment in a range of industrial and commercial developments. It still has a reliance on the mining sector, but today it's less of a boom-bust town and more of a regional city with a future. And notwithstanding its industrial image, it's a coastal town with beaches and easy access to Great Barrier Reef islands. And in 2020 it was a cheap place to buy houses. It has recorded prodigious growth recently – suburbs such as Kin Kora and New Auckland lifted 25% to 30% in FY2025.

Other notable markets – the future performers

That list charting price growth over the previous five years was published early in 2025. If they created such a list in 2027, the leading locations would be different because of the ebbs and flows of market locations. Remember that real estate is local, and while one location is rising, another will be flatlining, having reached the peak of its current cycle.

But while the names on the 2027 list might be different, the characteristics will be similar. Some will have featured on the 2025 list but outside of the top 10 – locations that got on a growth path later than Murray Bridge and Gympie, which had started their rise around 2020.

Here are some of the places likely to feature on a 2026 or 2027 national top 10.

Albury–Wodonga, NSW/Vic.

This important and strategic regional centre has the almost-unique characteristic of functioning as one city across two states. It's an important location logistically because of its proximity to Sydney, Canberra and Melbourne. Many big businesses have distribution centres there. The economy is strong and diverse, and it's on the route of the $31 billion Inland Rail link connecting Melbourne to Brisbane. Its lifestyle elements include the Murray River, Lake Hume and nearby mountain regions. It's had big value growth in recent years and would likely make a national top 10 list for five-year uplift in 2026 or 2027.

If you're motivated to buy in Albury–Wodonga, keep in mind that buying north of the state border will involve much lower stamp duty and land tax.

Blacktown City, NSW

The suburb of Blacktown and the municipality of the same name defy many of the myths that clutter the real estate air waves. It's stigmatised as a downmarket problem area a long way from the Sydney CBD, yet Blacktown and neighbouring suburbs have long-term growth rates above 10% per year.

The reality is that the Western Sydney economy is one of the nation's success stories, and from that has sprung real estate growth. Blacktown has good infrastructure – including motorway and rail connections, a hospital, a university campus and massive employment nodes nearby – and government spending has enhanced this in recent years, with plenty more to come. Its proximity to the new Western Sydney International Airport and the surrounding aerotropolis will provide further impetus.

This precinct is a major target for first-home buyers because it's affordable (by Sydney standards) and has been often a state leader on grants to first-home buyers. The suburb of Blacktown recorded around 500 house sales in FY2025, and its median price topped $1 million, but there remain suburbs in the LGA with house price medians in the $700,000s and $800,000s.

Brisbane (inner), Qld

Greater Brisbane has been one of the nation's growth markets since 2023, buoyed by a strong economy, big infrastructure spending and internal migration bringing new residents to Queensland. Its prices have overtaken Melbourne and it's likely to keep on rising, with the 2032 Summer Olympics poised to generate more momentum. Studies of cities that have hosted the Games show an undeniable impact on real estate, primarily in the years preceding the event, because of the massive investment in infrastructure to get ready. History also suggests that the suburbs closest to the main Olympics venues receive the greatest uplift – and in Brisbane's case that means the suburbs clustered around the CBD. This runs counter to the testimony elsewhere in the book that precincts close to the CBD are no longer the big performers on growth – but these are special circumstances. The Olympics are set to make this one of the nation's great lifestyle precincts. Significant lifestyle features have evolved in riverside precincts such as South Bank, New Farm and Hamilton, giving inner Brisbane major lifestyle appeal at relatively affordable prices, particularly with apartments.

Bunbury, WA

The second largest city in Western Australia finished just outside the top 10 in the 2025 report by CoreLogic. It got onto a major growth path in 2022 and had three stellar years thereafter. Its most affordable suburbs, Carey Park and Withers, have averaged 19% to 20% per year growth in their median prices over the past five years. Bunbury offers a seaside lifestyle, investment in major infrastructure (including the $1.25 billion ring road), affordable homes and a price-to-yield ratio that attracted investors from 2022 to 2025. Many Bunbury suburbs recorded growth of 30% or higher in FY2025. The city has the underlying credentials to be a growth market long term, beyond the recent boom period, including proximity to Perth and relative affordability.

Burnie, Tas.

Burnie is the Tasmanian version of the kind of places that led the nation on rising property values between 2020 and 2025: small, little-known regional centres with diverse economies, investment in business enterprises and infrastructure, lifestyle benefits and affordable dwellings. This northern coastal centre has an important export port that also welcomes cruise ships, and it's the centre of a renewable energy zone attracting state government investment. Regional Tasmania was identified by PIPA research as the number one jurisdiction in Australia for price growth in the 20 years to 2024 and was showing signs of moving into another growth phase in 2025, alongside a recovering Hobart market. Suburbs of Burnie have median house prices in the $300,000s and $400,000s, and several of them have long-term growth averages around 10% or 12% per year.

Darwin, NT

Late in 2024 my analysis of forward-looking data detected the first stirrings of a revival in the long-dormant Darwin market. A national analysis of infrastructure investment revealed that Darwin had the biggest per capita spend in the works of all the market jurisdictions in the nation. There were indications of improvement in the stuttering Northern Territory economy. The city's lifestyle offering included a warm winter climate. It had the lowest prices and the highest rental yields of the eight state and territory capital cities. Sales activity was starting to rise. Within six months, it had become the hottest market in Australia. As a small city that is strategically important for resources and defence, it's had a boom-bust history, but at the time of writing its future looks very positive. It would feature high on a national top 10 list published in 2026 or 2027.

Frankston, Vic.

The Melbourne market overall was in the doldrums when smaller cities were booming in 2023 and 2024. There were signs of revival late in 2024 and early in 2025, led by the City of Frankston, which quickly became one of the hottest markets in Greater Melbourne.

The suburb of Frankston and others in the LGA of the same name have much to offer: a bayside setting, motorway and rail links to Melbourne, lots of amenities (including extensive green space) and relative affordability. The big kicker is work on another of those billion-dollar hospital projects that are so influential in real estate. Buyer demand has been rising strongly, and the Winter 2025 edition of Hotspotting's *Price Predictor Index* featured three Frankston LGA suburbs in its *National Top 50 List of Supercharged Suburbs*.

Geelong, Vic.

It's amazing how wrong the media can be in focusing on the bad and ignoring the good. Geelong was deemed to have a bleak future when many of the old industries were closing. Media hysteria reached new levels when the Holden car plant shut down in 2016. It was around that time that I was including the City of Greater Geelong in my *Hotspots* reports. The report on Geelong had a long list of new infrastructure projects, business ventures and property developments. We could see that the jobs being created in the new ventures massively outnumbered the jobs being lost in the car plant closure.

I was strongly recommending Geelong as an investment choice in 2017. Geelong, I thought, had a big future as an affordable lifestyle alternative to Melbourne. The local economy was transitioning successfully from the old industries to the new ones, with the health and education sectors now the biggest employers. The Regional Rail Link, opened in 2015, improved transport from Geelong to central Melbourne. The recommended suburbs of Geelong were mostly on the Bellarine Peninsula, with access to water-based lifestyle amenities. And they were affordable relative to Melbourne. Three years later, in 2020, many of its suburbs had recorded exceptional growth in their property prices.

In 2025 there were indications that Geelong was entering a new growth phase. It was highlighted in the June 2025 edition of the *Regional Movers Index* as the number one destination in Australia for internal migrants, overtaking the Sunshine Coast.

Logan City, Qld

Elsewhere in this book I record the exceptional value uplift experienced in the suburbs of this vast municipality, which includes boom-level growth in median unit prices recently. Logan encompasses the southern suburbs of Greater Brisbane, providing the urban bridge between central Brisbane and the Gold Coast, which are connected by rail links and the M1, soon to be replicated by a new motorway. The Gateway Motorway and the Logan Motorway intersect with the M1 in Logan, so it's a nerve centre for transport links in south-east Queensland. The LGA includes a major medical precinct and university campus, lots of commercial and industrial precincts, big retail along the route of the M1 and a surprisingly large number of golf courses. If you like the Gold Coast but can't afford to buy there, neighbouring Logan is a good option.

As Brisbane rises in the lead-up to the 2032 Summer Olympics, Logan City will be dragged along with that momentum and its own good qualities.

Melbourne (inner), Vic.

Three factors were giving momentum to the inner-city areas of Melbourne in 2025:

1. the general upturn in the Victorian market after a couple of slow years that left Greater Melbourne with prices cheaper than Brisbane, much cheaper than Sydney and Canberra,

and on a par with Adelaide and Perth – and therefore good value for money

2. an improving economy, high population growth (mostly overseas migrants) and big infrastructure investment

3. the rise and rise of apartments – suburbs in the City of Melbourne LGA, including Carlton, Kensington, North Melbourne and the CBD, were recording rising buyer demand in 2025, helped by proximity to city offices, two big university campuses and a major hospitals precinct.

The Winter 2025 edition of the *Price Predictor Index* nominated the City of Melbourne as one of the nation's rising markets – for investors able to disregard the high taxes and generally unfriendly demeanour of the Victorian state government towards them.

Mount Gambier, SA

South Australia's largest population centre outside Adelaide was 20th on the post-COVID list, growing 72% in the five years. The numbers will look stronger in a year or two. It's roughly equi-distant from Adelaide and Melbourne; it has several economic engines pumping, including tourism, forestry, manufacturing and renewable energy; it offers a country lifestyle close to the coast; and it has lots of affordable dwellings. New residents have been moving there, and investors have discovered it for its affordability and solid yields. Competition from growing numbers of buyers has put upward pressure on prices, which have been rising steadily since 2021. In four years, the median house price moved from $280,000 to $500,000. It's a regional city with a strong future, and it has that combination of economy, lifestyle and affordability that will attract buyers and drive prices still higher.

Rockhampton, Qld

This central Queensland city was always destined to become a boom market. The vibrant local economy and the "exodus to affordable lifestyle" trend has brought new residents to Rockhampton, and in 2024 and 2025 it became an investor target because prices were low, yields were high and future growth prospects looked good. Typical houses in the riverside suburb of Berserker cost $250,000 in mid-2022, and three years later they were $430,000. When the market was at its most frenzied, houses were selling as fast as vendors could list them, with dozens of buyers competing for individual properties. The city's economy is diverse, comprising manufacturing, tourism, military, agriculture, resources and renewable energy, and multiple billions are being invested in new infrastructure, including the ring road, a major water pipeline and the Shoalwater Bay Training Area. This suggests that long-term growth is part of Rockhampton's future.

Salisbury or Playford, SA

The northern suburbs of Adelaide have featured at various points throughout this book because they present a great case for buying in downmarket locations with good amenities, infrastructure investment, major employment nodes and affordable dwellings regardless of what the real estate snobs would say. The capital growth rates in recent years have been extraordinary, vacancies have been ultra-low, and rents have grown strongly. Most people who bought there in 2020 would have more than doubled their money by 2025. Just as one example, the suburb of Para Hills lifted its median house price from $340,000 to over $700,000 in five years.

There are dozens of similar examples. At the time of writing, there was no sign of the growth in values slowing down. Underpinning it all is one of Australia's strongest state economies.

Sunshine Coast, Qld

I rate the Sunshine Coast among the strongest economic and real estate stories in the nation. It has transitioned from a tourist town with a struggling property market to one of Australia's major growth cities – one with pretensions to be regarded as an international city.

It's a case study of how investment in infrastructure can be the ultimate game-changer. Around 2020 the Sunshine Coast was in the midst of rolling out an infrastructure pipeline totalling $20 billion: a world-class medical precinct based around the $2 billion Sunshine Coast University Hospital (SCUH); transformation of the local airport into an international gateway; a subsea internet cable link to Asia; multi-billion-dollar investment in roadways; expansion of major retail facilities; creation of a CBD with hotel, office, retail and residential components; and considerably more. From 2020 to 2023 the Sunshine Coast was a national leader in price growth. Home values in upmarket suburbs doubled in three years, boosted by the influx of new residents employed by SCUH.

Although tourism remains an important industry to the Sunshine Coast, its economy is insulated by the evolving medical precinct, the ongoing construction of the CBD and population growth, for which the region consistently ranks in the national top 10. Its involvement in the 2032 Summer Olympics will lead to further major investment, with a rail link to the coast a high priority. It also continues to be one of the leading beneficiaries of internal migration.

Toowoomba, Qld

I've referenced Australia's second largest inland city numerous times in this book for its many special qualities. Its median house price rose 73% from 2020 to 2025 and it's sure to become one of those places where property values double in five years. Toowoomba ticks all the boxes: a multi-faceted economy, a growing population, big infrastructure projects, lifestyle features and affordable dwellings.

Two transport infrastructure events have put Toowoomba on the map nationally (and internationally): a new airport with direct flights to Sydney and Melbourne, and the $31 billion Inland Rail link, for which Toowoomba is the main Queensland hub. This has inspired businesses to target major ventures on land close to the airport and rail hub. Additional economic impetus will come from construction of a billion-dollar hospital, which will operate in addition to the existing major hospital. This is a recipe for why property values rise.

Townsville, Qld

It's a sure bet that a five-year growth list in a year or two will have Townsville a lot higher than its 28th place in 2025. Townsville has been a leading growth market from 2023 to 2025, with many suburbs recording 25% to 30% increases in their median house prices in a single year. This is one of the nation's strongest regional economies, with major contributions from tourism, military, resources, education, medical, manufacturing and government administration. It's the unofficial capital of Far North Queensland, with a big government presence, a world-class stadium to host sports and music events, a major university, an army base and a Royal Australian Air Force (RAAF) facility. Many big mining companies active in Queensland have a corporate presence in

Townsville. It entered its latest growth phase offering affordable homes, attracting new residents as well as investors. It gets whacked by tropical weather events every so often, and that means insurance costs are high, but buyers don't seem to care.

Wollongong, NSW

The Illawarra region is an important economy to New South Wales, headed by Wollongong and supported by the Shoalhaven and Shellharbour LGAs. It has transitioned successfully from the old economy to a modern one, with the education, medical and IT sectors now important, as well as tourism and the region's export port at Port Kembla.

Being close to Sydney and being seen as a relatively affordable lifestyle alternative to the big city is important. As more Sydney residents seek options outside of Australia's most expensive city – but not too far away – Wollongong and nearby towns will gain new residents, putting further upward pressure on prices. The City of Wollongong LGA featured strongly in the Winter 2025 edition of the *Price Predictor Index*, as did neighbouring Shoalhaven, which includes the important town of Nowra, with its major naval base and an expanding hospital.

Chapter 11

Leading indicators

There's a big difference between lagging indicators and leading indicators. The media talks mainly about lagging indicators. They tell you what happened in the past. My business is essentially interested in leading indicators, the ones that tell you what will likely happen in the future.

You won't read much about forward-looking metrics in *The Australian* or *The Age*, or in the many online "magazines" that regurgitate press releases as news. Journalists focus largely on median price data and auction clearance rates; they are regarded as the key barometers of the state of markets. However, they tell you very little that's useful if you're trying to decide where to buy.

Median prices can be a very blunt instrument for measuring real estate markets. They're often full of aberrations. It's common to see media outlets publish lists of what they describe as the "Top 10 Suburbs for Capital Growth", but they haven't weeded out the anomalies, often caused by small sales samples. I've seen such lists contain locations that have recorded only two sales in the past year; you cannot, by definition, have a median price when there have been only two sales. I've seen locations on these lists that have recorded no residential sales at all because they're rural or industrial areas, yet somehow they make a list spat out of a computer that no one bothered to check before firing it off to the media.

Even if we overlook the statistical glitches that abound, a list of suburbs that have recorded the highest increases in median prices in the past year doesn't tell a prospective investor anything useful. It may be interesting, but it's not news you can use. The past does not inform the future. It tells you where you should have bought two years ago, not where you should buy today. If the median price has jumped 40% in the past three years, you'd be silly to buy there now, because you missed the boat. You want a location with similar qualities that hasn't yet had that kind of growth.

Equally, a location that has performed poorly in the past may well be the best place for you to buy today. Change is a constant in real estate.

If you base investment decisions on past performance, you would not have invested in Sydney in 2013. It had been the great underachiever of Australian real estate for 10 years, with few growth spurts. But the smart money was buying there ahead of the boom that was to come. They were using leading indicators that suggested an up-cycle was looming – and soon, Sydney was booming.

If you base investment decisions on past performance, you would not have invested in the Sunshine Coast in 2017. It had a poor recent record on capital growth, having been a struggling economy overly reliant on a fickle tourism industry. But the forward-looking indicators I use suggested this was a good place to buy. Previously, the Sunshine Coast featured in my regular *No Go Zones* reports, but I started including it in *Hotspots* reports. I could see what was coming. Big game-changing events were happening. It's become one of the most compelling growth stories anywhere in Australia.

Rents up but prices dormant

David McMillan is the founder and director of Melbourne advisory Performance Property. He worked for a number of property firms, studying real estate investment techniques, before deciding on methodology he considered the best of all the things he had learnt. Today, Performance Property's team of over 100 staff members services high-income individuals who want to invest in growth markets ahead of the pack.

One marker of future price growth revealed by his research was a period of strong rental growth but no significant price growth. That was the state of play in Sydney in 2011 and 2012 – rents rose but prices did little. At that point, Performance Property started buying in Sydney for their clients. What followed was five years of extensive price growth.

This factor was also apparent in Hobart in 2016 and 2017. The lowest vacancies of any capital city in Australia led to big rental movements, which were then followed by three years in which prices grew in double digits each year.

This is an important barometer of our major markets that is overlooked by the mainstream media. I see movements in rents as more important than changes in median prices and auction clearance rates – because they're a forward-looking indicator. They reveal a lot about the state of play in individual markets, and they can serve as a precursor of what's likely to happen with prices.

Hobart still had the tightest vacancies of any capital city in Australia in mid-2020, and it continued to lead on rent increases.

And prices were still growing, regardless of the pandemic. However, by this metric, Perth was the city of greatest interest in mid 2020. Vacancies were low and rents were rising, against a backdrop of six years of declining property prices. In October 2020, Perth was the national leader on rental growth by a considerable margin, but overall prices had not yet moved. At the time, I wrote, "If history repeats, this dramatic improvement in the Perth rental market will be followed by uplift in sales prices for the first time since 2014". Perth went on to lead the nation on price growth.

Adelaide, too, was producing solid rental growth on the back of very low vacancy rates. The South Australian capital had been producing price growth in recent years, but the average growth rates across the city were moderate only – 2% or 3%. It was overdue for an up-cycle, and the situation with vacancies and rents suggested the time was nigh. From 2020 Adelaide started delivering consistently strong growth in property values, which extended through to 2025.

This is a simple but effective method of identifying future growth markets. As David McMillan says, "Sometimes people overcomplicate real estate. The essence of it is quite simple".

Vacancy rates low

Vacancy rates are the most underrated and underreported of all the parameters that chart real estate markets.

Here's a simplistic view of why they matter: if vacancies are low, rents will rise. And as I have just shown, when rents rise, prices tend to follow. It works in reverse as well: locations with high vacancies seldom deliver price growth. This makes trends in vacancy rates really important.

The trends late in 2020 suggested rising rents and, ultimately, prices in many locations around Australia. SQM Research's monthly report on vacancy rates for the eight state and territory capital cities showed in August 2020 that, for the third month in a row, there were notable reductions in vacancies. In April 2020 the national average vacancy rate was 2.6%. In May, it dropped to 2.5%. In June, it fell further to 2.2% and by July it was 2.1%.

Significantly, in June 2020 vacancies fell in all eight capital cities, and in July vacancies fell again in seven of the eight capital cities. In five of the eight capitals, vacancies were now below 1.5%. At the same time, most regional centres also had tight rental markets. Dubbo's vacancy rate was 0.7% and falling. Orange's was 0.4% and falling. Vacancies were below 1% in most Bendigo postcodes and trending lower. All the postcodes in Ballarat were below 2% and falling. And all the towns of the Latrobe Valley were under 1% and going down. The most recent figures from both SQM and the Real Estate Institute of Queensland (REIQ) confirmed that central Queensland towns and cities had very low vacancies and rising rentals.

The overwhelming conclusion was that there was a shortage of rental properties across Australia overall, despite all the impacts of the pandemic, and as a consequence, rents were increasing.

It was significant that the cities and regional areas with low vacancies were places where the pandemic was under control. Restrictions were relaxed, people were getting on with business and real estate markets were busy. There was upward pressure on prices in many of these places, helped by improved confidence in all those parts of Australia that exist outside of Sydney and Melbourne – which, keep in mind, is where the majority of Australians live.

Sales activity rising

The mainstream media defines real estate markets by movements in median prices. The median price figures published by the major research firms and regurgitated by the news media are generalised in nature. They provide a single figure to describe the Sydney market – for example, Sydney house prices have increased 3% in the past 12 months.

Think about the size of Greater Sydney and the diversity of its 600-plus suburbs. In a typical year there are 60,000 or 70,000 dwelling sales across the Sydney metropolitan area. To distil all of that into a single figure which purports to describe the Sydney market can lead to misleading analysis. In FY2025, when Sydney values rose perhaps 2% or 3% according to the generalised numbers, there were suburban clusters that recorded double-digit growth.

Another problem is that median prices are historical data. A report describing a 10% rise in a city's median price in the past 12 months is not particularly helpful to consumers, because the rise has already happened.

There's also a time lag with prices. Markets change long before prices do. It takes time for a change in activity at the coalface to deliver a reaction in prices. That's true both for rising and falling markets.

Sales activity data is far more revealing – and in terms of prices, it's a leading indicator. The most valuable and insightful report published by my Hotspotting business is the *Price Predictor Index*, which is based on analysis of trends in sales activity for every suburb and town in Australia.

Here's what I know to be true based on 40-plus years of research and experience: if sales volumes are rising steadily, prices will rise; if sales activity is falling, prices will stop rising and may fall. It sounds simplistic, but it works. The key factor is that there's a time lag before the median price data reacts to a change in sales activity – which makes analysis of sales volumes a forward indicator of price movements.

My business examines the raw data on sales volumes every quarter for every suburb and town in Australia. We don't chart the number of sales in Sydney; we monitor sales activity in Chipping Norton, Epping, Manly, Rouse Hill and Blacktown. We're not so much interested in how many homes are selling, quarter by quarter, in Greater Melbourne; we want to know the trends in St Kilda, Footscray, Box Hill, Cranbourne, Werribee and Melton. We want to know what's happening in suburban clusters, with a focus on LGAs. Real estate markets are very local in nature; the upmarket Brisbane suburb of New Farm may be pumping but downmarket Caboolture may be tanking, and the pattern for Penrith may contrast the trend in Bondi Beach. The Winter 2025 edition of the *Price Predictor Index* found that the overall numbers for Greater Melbourne were lukewarm, but the data on the LGAs of Frankston, Mornington Peninsula, Moonee Valley and the City of Melbourne was compelling, showing significant uplift (which was confirmed by anecdotal evidence at the time).

A price boom in Sydney ended – as a generalisation – in 2017. The media reacted with customary shock and horror, but I was telling our clients it was coming long before it showed up in the median price data. I could see it in the sales volumes: Sydney peaked in 2015 and gradually faded throughout 2016. It took time to show up in the median price data, as it always does, because median prices lag behind the game.

The end of the 2020 to 2021 COVID boom showed up in the sales data late in 2021 and early in 2022, but it wasn't evident in the median price statistics until later. The RBA started lifting the official interest rate in May 2022, and economists, who see everything through the interest-rate prism, postulated that the end of the up-cycle was caused by the first of the interest-rate rises, but the downturn started much earlier.

The explosion in the Darwin market in 2025, first evidenced in price data around May 2025, was forewarned by a notable upturn in sales numbers in the December 2024 quarter and then again, more starkly, in the March 2025 quarter. We were writing about it many months before the news media noticed it.

Infrastructure spending – the mother of all markers

Sydney and Melbourne (generally speaking) boomed between 2013 and 2017. The media proclaimed a national property boom. But only the two biggest cities excelled. Brisbane didn't, nor did Adelaide or Perth, or most of regional Australia. Why was it so?

One stark difference between the big two and the rest stands out: during that period, Sydney and Melbourne experienced massive spending on new infrastructure. Tens of billions of dollars were being spent on rail links, motorways, tunnels, hospitals and universities. During that same period, infrastructure development in Brisbane, Adelaide and Perth was at a standstill.

Coincidence? Not at all. There is an undeniable link between infrastructure spending and rising property markets. Infrastructure spending catalyses property markets in two major ways: it generates economic activity and jobs, and it improves the amenity of locations. Out of that arises demand for real estate.

For anyone seeking a simple philosophy to underpin their investment strategy, here's a good one: follow the infrastructure trail. Buy property that lies in the path of progress. The cost of many infrastructure projects is measured in billions of dollars, so their impact can be considerable.

Right now, Australia has more big infrastructure projects underway than ever before. The response of governments across the nation to the economic impacts of COVID lockdowns and restrictions was to bring forward big-ticket projects that would create jobs, put money into business bank accounts and improve the lives of communities. At the start of 2025, I researched projects under construction or in planning and found that the cost of these projects nationwide was over $900 billion. That doesn't include projects to build houses or apartments – just the infrastructure enterprises.

This unprecedented level of infrastructure development has major impacts on the housing crisis, exacerbating the housing shortage and the affordability problem. The big infrastructure projects attract tradespeople who would normally be working on home construction. A shortage of tradies is a big part of the housing shortage problem and one of many reasons why the cost of building homes is so high. The big infrastructure projects also elevate housing demand during construction and in the ultimate operation of the facilities, putting further pressure on property prices.

In researching capital growth rates of suburbs in the major cities of Australia, I've found a clear pattern: suburbs with commuter train stations have higher growth rates than those without. So, it's unsurprising that when a new rail link is created, suburbs that previously lacked commuter train services, and now have them, experience price growth. New or upgraded motorway links can have a similar impact.

Currently, the biggest national infrastructure project is the Inland Rail link, most recently costed at $31 billion and likely to cost more by completion. It's being built in stages, with the first of its 13 components officially launched in December 2018, and it will ultimately connect Melbourne to Brisbane via regional

New South Wales. Some sections have already been completed at the time of writing, and there has been notable uplift in real estate activity and prices in locations where work has been underway, including Parkes and Moree in New South Wales.

Key centres along the route of the Inland Rail link include Albury–Wodonga at the Victoria–New South Wales border; Wagga Wagga, Parkes, Narrabri and Moree in New South Wales; and Toowoomba in Queensland. When this game-changing project is completed – no one in politics and bureaucracy is willing to commit to an end date – locations along the route will gain additional impetus in their local property markets.

In Sydney, nowhere fits the philosophy of buying property that lies in the path of progress better than Western Sydney. A major share of the infrastructure underway or in planning for the Greater Sydney area is focused on Western Sydney, inspired by the construction of the new airport at Badgerys Creek.

Western Sydney is Australia's third largest economy, housing almost half of Greater Sydney's total population and producing 31% of Sydney's gross regional product (GRP). At around $100 billion, it's 8% of the national gross domestic product (GDP). Over the past decade the Western Sydney population has grown faster than the rest of Sydney's population and is likely to continue to do so, given the availability of land for new communities and the drawcard provided by the new airport.

The key thing about a major city airport is the commercial-industrial hub it creates. In all our cities, the airport is surrounded by businesses with reasons to be nearby. The Western Sydney airport and the associated aerotropolis is set to become the biggest employment node in the Greater Sydney metro area, and people will always want to live as close as possible to where they work – the research shows this is a key factor in where people choose to buy or rent. So, residential property markets in neighbouring municipalities like Liverpool, Blacktown and Penrith will be boosted.

According to the definition in a NAB report, Greater Western Sydney extends from Canterbury-Bankstown in the east to the Blue Mountains in the west, and from Hawkesbury in the north to Wollondilly in the south, and comprises 13 LGAs. It is expected to absorb two-thirds of the future population growth of the Sydney region.

Because of the magnitude of the growth expected, the Western Sydney City Deal has been put together in a partnership between the federal government, the state government and the local governments of the Blue Mountains, Camden, Campbelltown, Fairfield, Hawkesbury, Liverpool, Penrith and Wollondilly. The creation of new infrastructure is a fundamental piece of Greater Western Sydney's growth plans, with projects worth $35 billion in the pipeline. The deal includes creating the "30-minute city" through the delivery of the North South Rail Line and other connective infrastructure, including major new road and rail links, as well as contributing to 200,000 jobs through the aerotropolis.

Private investment opportunities will abound as Sydney's new aerotropolis development takes off. Precincts focused on agribusiness and manufacturing are expected to be up and running by the time the airport opens in December 2026. Businesses in those sectors have committed to build facilities in the area, including advanced 3D-printing company Colibrium Additive; Australian vitamin and pharmaceutical maker Vitex; the Australian Space Agency, aerospace company Northrop Grumman (which has committed to a $50 million investment in an advanced defence electronics maintenance and sustainment centre) and 18 small to medium enterprises (SMEs) in the aerospace industry; and Sydney Markets, the state's largest wholesale produce market. Japanese multinationals Mitsubishi Heavy Industries and the Sumitomo Mitsui Financial Group have also agreed to invest in the aerotropolis.

These and other big-ticket projects underway or planned for Western Sydney potently drive demand for housing, and price growth over time is inevitable in the LGAs of Blacktown, Liverpool and Penrith, with the momentum spreading further south to Campbelltown and Camden. Many suburbs throughout these precincts already have good track records in delivering capital growth – most suburbs in the Blacktown LGA, for example, have long-term growth rates (the average over the past five years) between 10% and 12% per year (which means values doubling in six or seven years), well above Greater Sydney norms.

Education–medical infrastructure

Perhaps the most influential form of infrastructure on real estate is hospitals. A $1 billion hospital can create many thousands of jobs in construction and 5000 or 6000 in operations. The number and size of medical facilities under development or expansion in Australia currently is without precedent, and they will have a game-changing impact on local economies and property markets.

In major cities across Australia, universities and hospitals tend to cluster together. The North Melbourne–Parkville precinct in Melbourne is a prime example. The North Ryde precinct in Sydney is another, as is the Murdoch precinct in Perth, Kelvin Grove–Herston in Brisbane, the Loganlea area in Brisbane, the Westmead–Parramatta precinct in Sydney, and Southport on the Gold Coast. Universities and hospitals are a natural associates. Sometimes a new medical facility is specifically labelled a "university hospital".

When a new hospital is built, it's a big deal; it can be more influential than a new motorway or rail link. Transport infrastructure creates thousands of jobs in construction but very few in the post-construction operational phase. Hospitals and universities are different – they create lots of employment in construction but even more in their ongoing operation. A big-city hospital commonly can employ 5000 or 6000 people. A cluster of universities and hospitals, then, is a goldmine for the local property market, because people want to live close to where they're working or studying.

As I report elsewhere in this book, the Sunshine Coast economy was transformed by a $20 billion program of infrastructure developments, with the $2 billion Sunshine Coast University Hospital (SCUH) – part of a $5 billion medical precinct that created a whole new industry for the Sunshine Coast – the most influential. Around 6000 people work there. Keep in mind that this is in addition to existing medical facilities in the region; the biggest facility prior to SCUH was Nambour General Hospital, which continues to be a very busy facility. While SCUH was the centrepiece, other facilities sprung up around it, including a private hospital, specialist medical centres and a hotel. Dwelling values in the Sunshine Coast – including Noosa, which had been stagnant for 10 years prior – have been elevated since SCUH opened in 2017. The top end of the Sunshine Coast market – including Sunshine Beach, Noosa and Minyama, recorded extraordinary price rises, with prices doubling in three years. SCUH is not the only factor, but it is one of biggest.

The $730 million Tweed Valley Hospital opened in northern New South Wales in May 2024, not far from the intersection of the M1 and the Tweed Coast Road. In nearby Kingscliff, where property values had been flat in the previous two years, the median house price rose 11% in the 12 months following completion. Kingscliff's vacancy rate was 0.7%, one of the lowest in the region. The apartment market in nearby Casuarina rose 27%. Tweed Heads house values increased 16%, well above the location's five-year growth average. The new hospital is not the only factor at play in these markets, which are popular lifestyle locations, but it is a major new element.

Tweed Valley Hospital is close to the Kingscliff TAFE campus, which introduces another particularly powerful factor of infrastructure impact in generating real estate demand: the co-location of medical and educational facilities.

The City of Marion in Adelaide is one of Australia's best examples of how a cluster of medical, educational and innovation facilities can turbocharge property values. The Flinders University campus sits in Bedford Park alongside the Flinders Medical Centre, which includes Flinders Private Hospital, the Flinders University College of Medicine and Public Health, Laurel Hospice and a lot more. A stone's throw away is the Tonsley Innovation District, repurposing what was once a Mitsubishi car plant, which includes a TAFE SA campus and an extension of the Flinders University campus. Given the additional presence of the M2, rail links, major shopping centres and sporting and recreational amenities, it's a salient case study on what happens when all the big infrastructure pieces of the puzzle are in place.

Residential suburbs in the precinct have experienced steadily rising house values for the past five years. The Hotspotting research hub shows all the surrounding suburbs have five-year growth averages of 13% or 14%, which means values doubling in five or six years. Vacancy rates below 1% are common in this precinct, with annual rental growth above 10%. House values in the suburb of Marion lifted 26% in the 12 months to May 2025, with houses typically selling in 20 days. Mitchell Park rose 14%, with houses selling on average in 19 days and the vacancy rate at 0.5%. Bellevue Heights rose 13% in 12 months, with zero vacancies and an average time on market of 19 days.

It needs to be recorded that Greater Adelaide generally has been a growth market for many years, and other parts of the city have delivered strong value growth. The key point, however, is that the suburbs in this hotbed of infrastructure elements have outperformed city norms on value escalation. The City of Marion, which encompasses most of the suburbs mentioned (Bellevue Heights is in the neighbouring Mitcham LGA), is a perennial growth leader in Adelaide. My analysis of sales activity in the March 2025 quarter found that the Marion suburbs were again a standout, with rising buyer demand pointing to further growth in property values.

Spending on *new* infrastructure is the big kicker

Often newspapers and magazines will ask real estate professionals to nominate the suburbs they think will show big growth in the coming year. It's a popular feature every new year.

When a real estate agent names a particular suburb as a looming hotspot and is asked why, the answer is along these lines: "It's got lots of good streetscapes, it has schools, there's a major shopping centre, lots of café culture, it's on the train line and it's close to the motorway into the city".

Yes, great – those are all solid credentials. But that suburb has long had those features. It had those qualities last year, and five years ago, and 20 years ago. Why will those qualities cause it to boom this year? What has changed to convert this solid suburb into the hotspot of the year? Nothing. So, why will it boom?

The best places to buy can be places that have those solid core qualities *and* something new in the mix –game-changing events such as a new rail link, a new university campus, a new commercial estate bringing new jobs to the area or, ideally, all of the above. The ideal location can be a suburb with excellent existing infrastructure – a place with good real estate bones – but also new infrastructure investment in the pipeline. This is what made the Sunshine Coast a national leader on house price growth from 2020 to 2023.

Toowoomba had solid credentials and then became a boom location through transport infrastructure investment: the $1.6 billion Second Range Crossing and the new Wellcamp Airport. It will go to another level when the $31 billion Inland Rail link comes to town and the $1.2 billion hospital is completed. It's as close to a stone-cold certainty as you can get in real estate.

Why are the suburbs of the City of Marion in Adelaide still delivering? It's in large part because the infrastructure landscape in this area keeps evolving. The Tonsley Innovation Precinct is constantly expanding, with new educational facilities and residential developments. The Flinders University campus at Bedford Park will be expanded with a $1.5 billion Flinders Village project, which includes more health research facilities, student accommodation and a hotel. A $280 million health research facility opened in 2024 as part of a larger, multi-stage expansion. A $140 million extension to the rail link will make access easier.

Nothing turbocharges real estate values long term like this kind of infrastructure investment.

Chapter 12

Lessons from the COVID boom

My business is involved in the science of detecting and analysing change, preferably before anyone else does. Real estate never sits still. Change is a constant. And sometimes the catalyst can be epic – with unexpected consequences.

The pandemic of 2020 provided a lesson in this. The onset was sudden, the impacts were monumental, and the outcomes caught most economists napping. While the media reported that certain locations had thriving markets "despite the pandemic", I thought it was more accurate to say "because of the pandemic".

I have commented extensively on the failure of high-profile economists to deliver credible analysis of, and accurate forecasts for, real estate. I have referenced their forecasts at the start of 2022, 2023 and 2024 that house prices would fall in the year ahead, only for them to be embarrassed by property markets across Australia. But the greatest failing of the faulty forecasters was the COVID boom. When the pandemic struck Australia early in 2020, economists began competing for media limelight with increasingly dire doomsday predictions about dwelling prices. In March/April 2020, ANZ economists Felicity Emmett and Adelaide Timbrell predicted a 13% decline in capital city prices. AMP Capital's Shane Oliver said house prices would fall 20% by the end of the year. Bill Evans of Westpac forecast a 10% drop in house prices in the next 12 months, while NAB said city prices would fall 10% to 15% in the next 12 months and 30% by the end of 2021. Gareth Aird of Commonwealth Bank released a series of possibilities: the best-case scenario was an 11% decline in Australian house prices, and the worst-case scenario was a 32% collapse on house prices in 2020. The level of decline expected by the brightest economic minds among the major banking institutions would have been unprecedented had it happened.

Even by the standard of the usual suspects in the forecasting industry, this was a stunning spectacle of misjudgment and failure to understand the forces at play. Hotspotting and other genuine real estate analysts like Simon Pressley of Propertyology were telling consumers to expect very different outcomes.

What unfolded was a real estate boom with few precedents in the nation's history. By the end of 2020 house prices had risen 6% nationally and 12% in Hobart, Darwin and regional Tasmania. Sydney rose 7% and Canberra 9%. In 2021 the national average was a 25% rise in house prices, with Sydney and Brisbane both increasing 30%.

In Sunshine Beach on the Sunshine Coast, the median house price rose from $1.8 million in mid-2020 to $3.3 million by the end of 2021. Nearby Noosa Heads apartments went from $915,000 to $1.6 million in two years, and another year later were $2 million. Byron Bay in New South Wales jumped from $1.5 million to $3.5 million in two years.

In more humble locations, the Geelong suburb of Corio increased from $365,000 in mid-2020 to $510,000 two years later. Flora Hill in Bendigo jumped from $380,000 to $560,000 in two years. Seaford in the south of Adelaide rose from $350,000 to $600,000 by the end of 2022 (and kept on rising). East Launceston in Tasmania increased from $570,000 in mid-2020 to over $900,000 by early 2023.

The shamefully bad advice given by economists in the first half of 2020 caused tens of thousands of Australians to miss the opportunity to invest for their families' future or cost them hundreds of thousands of dollars through delayed action. Those who were ready to buy homes in mid-2020 cancelled their plans because the media reports, fed by bank economists, said values would collapse. By the time they realised the opposite was happening, they had missed 20% to 30% growth in values in the properties they might otherwise have bought and had to pay so much more when they belatedly became buyers.

And when it became clear that a boom was happening, how did the economists rationalise it? They said it was because interest rates were at record lows. Kindergarten analysis.

Let's be crystal clear: cheap money didn't cause the COVID boom. Access to low-cost finance was part of the mix but not the key driver. Interest rates were at record lows in 2018 and 2019, but prices were falling in many locations across Australia. The multiple forces that generated the dramatic escalation in property prices in late 2020 and throughout 2021 had little to do with the cost of money.

The economy was stronger than expected, and unemployment never reached the highs predicted (another forecast the economists got wrong). State and federal government stimulus measures were highly influential. Governments brought forward investment in infrastructure to avoid recession. Support for first-home buyers was elevated. These and other factors created a revival in the resources sector.

Eventually, the build-up of savings during the lockdown periods became influential. There was pent-up demand in the system, which led to rising sales activity. That coincided with a shortage of homes on the market – listings were reduced because vendors had been told it was a really bad time to sell. Large numbers of expats returning from COVID hotspots overseas added to the rising buyer demand. Investors saw opportunities and so did foreign buyers, who saw Australia as a safe haven for their capital. The "exodus to affordable lifestyle" trend, which had been well underway before the pandemic arrived, was exacerbated by the COVID lockdowns.

One of the intangible factors that I believe important was the common perception of the safety and solidity of bricks and mortar in times of uncertainty. Real estate often thrives in times of economic disruption because Australians trust it with their money.

Now, let's consider indicators we examined in 2020 that suggested a boom was nigh. In September 2020, when economists and news media were still forecasting falling property values, I wrote a report identifying four significant trends that were pivotal for residential real estate, one or more (or all) of which were happening in the strongest markets:

1. The pandemic was pretty much under control and life (almost) back to normal.

2. First-home buyers were very active.

3. The "exodus to affordable lifestyle" trend was happening.

4. Vacancies were very low, putting upward pressure on rents.

Let's have a closer look at why these trends were happening and why they were important to real estate markets.

1. COVID back in its box

Deep into the pandemic period, real estate markets were busy in Perth, Adelaide, Canberra, Darwin, Brisbane and Hobart – much more so than in Sydney or Melbourne. Markets were also pumping in many of our major regional centres. Ballarat, Bendigo, Albury–Wodonga, Wagga Wagga, Dubbo, Orange, Newcastle, the Sunshine Coast, Mackay, Townsville, Alice Springs – many of these places were relatively untouched by the virus and less impacted by lockdowns. The median house price for Canberra rose every month from March to August 2020. Adelaide's median rose or was unchanged in five of those six months, based on CoreLogic data.

2. First-home buyers busy

The most active cohort in Australian real estate in 2020 was first-home buyers. It sounds like a real estate agents' pitch, but there had never been a better time to be a first-timer in Australia. Prices were subdued (but would not remain so for long), investors were sitting on the sidelines (so, less competition), the level of government assistance was the highest ever and the level of mortgage rates was the lowest ever.

Perfect storms don't come any better. The HomeBuilder grant was a particular catalyst, and young Australians were busily buying home sites with plans to build. In Perth, the number of residential land sales more than doubled between April and July in 2020.

All that buying activity put upward pressure on prices, particularly as supply was limited in many places. It made sense for investors to jump on board with this trend. First-home buyers buy in the cheaper areas, so investors could buy affordably in locations where prices were likely to rise.

3. The exodus to affordable lifestyle

Australians were making the choice to work remotely long before the pandemic brought lockdowns and enforced working from home. Technology made it increasingly possible, and in some cases, improved road or rail connections helped. The pandemic opened the eyes of more people (and their employers) to the possibilities of working outside of the traditional office environment.

This changed people's choices of where to live. Being in the big, congested, noisy and expensive city became less important, and more emphasis was given to a more relaxed and more affordable lifestyle. So, they started moving to the fringes of the big cities and beyond to hill-change and sea-change locations within an hour or two of their state capital.

Regional Victoria, in particular, came alive with refugees from Melbourne. Markets rose in Geelong and Ballarat initially, then Bendigo and the towns of the Latrobe Valley. It spread further out as well to regional centres like Shepparton, Warrnambool, Mildura, Wangaratta and Wodonga.

Regional locations within a couple of hours of Sydney started to rise. Wollongong, the Southern Highlands, the Blue Mountains, the Central Coast, Newcastle, Orange and the towns of the Hunter Valley were among the beneficiaries.

The Sunshine Coast in Queensland, already on the rise, gained further impetus from the trend. The Gold Coast, which has been a nation-leading population growth centre for decades, got some traction from this and from expats returning home because of the pandemic impact overseas.

The central theme was that we don't need to be in the big city anymore and we want a better lifestyle for less money. Sydney and Melbourne residents could sell their city homes, buy something of comparable standard for considerably less money in a regional location and have money in the bank.

The trend I call the "exodus to affordable lifestyle" has been evolving for over a decade; the official population statistics confirm that. It wasn't inspired by the pandemic, but it became more visible then and was certainly enhanced by the COVID restrictions. Media forecasts that the trend to the regions would reverse once COVID was dealt with have been proven inaccurate; the *Regional Movers Index* – which is published quarterly by Commonwealth Bank and the Regional Australia Institute and identifies the most popular destinations for people relocating from the big cities – shows that this demographic trend is continuing. Regional locations have been outperforming their state capital cities for many years. All of the leading locations for growth in property values since 2020 have been regional cities and towns.

4. Low vacancies almost everywhere

Journalists tend to be glass-half-empty people, so most media stories on vacancies in 2020 related to the sharp rise in empty apartments in inner-city areas (because Airbnb was no longer working in the closed-borders pandemic period). But these places were the exception to the overriding trend. Low vacancies were the norm across most of the nation, and in many places they were the lowest on record.

The industry benchmark for a balanced residential market with stable rents has long been a 3% vacancy rate. If it's above 3%, you're heading towards oversupply and rents may fall. If it's much below 3%, you have a shortage and rents are likely to rise. If it gets below 1%, you have tenants competing for scarce rentals and offering more than the asking rent.

In 2020, many locations across Australia had vacancies below 1%. Little changed over the next five years. In mid-2025, four of the eight capital cities still had vacancies well below 1% and the national average was around 1.2%.

I've written elsewhere in this book what history shows us about places where vacancies are low and rents are rising: prices tend to follow. A prolonged period of very low vacancies and rising rentals will often generate a property price boom.

Simon Pressley of Propertyology said in October 2020:

> We did some research on vacancies – large parts of Australia were really tight well before COVID. A report on the 50 biggest cities and towns showed only four had a vacancy rate over 3% – Sydney, Melbourne, Gold Coast, Geelong. Seventy-five percent of Australia's 50 biggest towns and cities were undersupplied – vacancies under 2%.

> In large parts of Australia, rents are rising. So, people buy – for example, first-home buyers. I call it "driving the market from the bottom up". It's a much more sustainable trend.

> For most of the last decade, Australia hasn't had anywhere near the level of investor activity that we had the decade before. Rental supply is a by-product of investor activity. This isn't new – markets have been driven by owner occupiers.

Chapter 13

Finding growth in unexpected places

You buy real estate for income and growth. For most, capital growth is nirvana. Your expectation might have been that your investment would double in value over 10 years. So, if you buy something and a decade later it's still worth pretty much the same, you're not a happy camper. You haven't made any money at all; indeed, in real terms you've lost money. So, the worst places to own real estate include the locations where values don't grow.

There are two problems with this, and they speak to key themes in this book: what most Australians think they know about property is wrong, and real estate is constantly changing.

An example of how things can change

Here's a quiz question from 2020: among the iconic real estate locations of Australia, which had the worst capital growth record – a place where the median price in 2020 was the same as it had been 10 years earlier?

The answer is Surfers Paradise – specifically, Surfers Paradise apartments.

Ironically, every year Surfers Paradise attracted thousands of buyers, mostly investors, who thought it was a great place to buy. Even big name, high-profile people who should know better were throwing money at high-rise units in the Gold Coast's most famous suburb during a time when it was a lame duck with no growth. At the time of writing Sussan Ley was the federal opposition leader with aspirations to be Prime Minister, but in 2017, when the Liberals were in power, she lost the Health Minister portfolio after being accused of misusing her travel allowance to go to Surfers Paradise to buy a high-rise apartment for $795,000. As I wrote in a newspaper column in January 2017, her biggest mistake was the investment itself. At the time, she said she bought the property because "the Gold Coast is a great place to invest". I wrote, "She clearly didn't do any research – there are few investments with worse records on capital growth than high-rise units on the Gold Coast".

At the time, Gold Coast high-rises were a regular inclusion in my *No Go Zones* reports. The potential for capital growth was suppressed by frequent bouts of oversupply. Developers constantly flooded the market with apartments in new mega-towers, and it often took years to absorb the surplus, which pushed down prices. Ley compounded her mistake by buying a Surfers Paradise high-rise at more than double the suburb's median price at the time, another investment no-no.

In September 2020 the median apartment price for Surfers Paradise was $375,000 according to CoreLogic data. The long-term growth rate (the average for the past 10 years) was zero. No change in values in a decade. The growth rate was only marginally better in neighbours like Main Beach (1.75% per year) and Broadbeach (1.2% per year). Investors like to think property doubles in value in 10 years (or less) but at a growth rate of 1.2% it would take 60 years. In nearby Southport, the long-term growth average in September 2020 was –0.2% – values were *lower* than 10 years earlier.

An investor with an inquiring mind might also wonder why apartments were so cheap in Surfers Paradise. The median of $375,000 compared with $750,000 at Main Beach, $590,000 at Coolangatta down at the New South Wales border and $440,000 at Maroochydore on the Sunshine Coast. Noosa Heads, another iconic location, was $870,000. The long-term growth rate at Noosa was 5% per year – still not great but way better than nothing.

The other ugly thing about Surfers Paradise was high vacancy rates. In mid-2020, they were fluctuating between 5% and 10%, hurt by the pandemic.

So many people thought it was great place to buy, but its capital growth performance was abysmal. How was it so? How did we have this disconnect between perception and reality?

Australians don't do a lot of research before tossing a lazy half million or more at a piece of real estate. They have a fundamental belief that real estate will grow no matter where you buy and in famous landmark locations like Surfers they will achieve spectacular growth. They overlook the oversupply factor – the one factor that can cause prices to fall in Australia.

But another key theme of this book is that real estate is constantly changing. The preceding commentary encapsulates the state of affairs in 2020. Five years on, it was very different. Surfers Paradise has become a performer on capital growth, as has the Gold Coast market generally. The one big negative that suppressed capital growth, oversupply, has been removed from the equation.

Big change started for the Gold Coast when the global pandemic occurred. Expats working overseas prepared to return by buying real estate back home, and the Gold Coast, particularly coastal high-rise, was high on the shopping list. The lockdown periods in the big capital cities of Australia also prompted many to buy on the Gold Coast. While many economists predicted Gold Coast property values would crash because its economy would tank without overseas tourists coming in, the opposite occurred – amid all the mayhem of the pandemic restrictions, the Gold Coast market boomed. Five years on, prices were still rising.

The Gold Coast has always had massive buyer demand. It has consistently featured among the population growth leaders of the nation. It has a lifestyle that appeals to many. In recent years, the infrastructure spend has been extensive, including upgrades and additions for the 2018 Commonwealth Games. There is the ongoing evolution of the light rail project, and the region's role in the 2032 Olympics will create further investment in infrastructure. Its economy relies on its tourism appeal, but it also has major economic sectors with education and medical services.

The only factor that constrained capital growth was oversupply from too many mega-towers adding thousands of apartments. But that has changed. The pandemic shortages curtailed developers' ability to build big projects, and then the rising cost of construction meant many projects became financially unviable. Now, the Gold Coast has the opposite problem: a serious shortage of dwellings.

The five years from 2020 to 2025 saw the Gold Coast become a notable performer on capital growth. The median apartment price for Surfers Paradise was around $770,000 in mid-2025, almost double the level of five years earlier. Southport, which lacks the glamour of Surfers but has important assets like a major hospital and a university campus, has grown at a faster rate, with the median prices for both houses and units averaging 14% growth per year over that five-year period. Nerang, at the base of the Gold Coast Hinterland on the motorway and the rail line to Brisbane, has averaged 14% growth per year for houses and 16% for units. There are similar numbers for suburbs across the Gold Coast region, with apartments usually outperforming houses on capital growth over five years.

The extraordinary resilience of local property markets

Australia is the land of natural disasters. It would be difficult to find anywhere in this vast land a location that has not been touched by storms, cyclones, floods, bushfires or drought. Easier to find are places that have suffered from climate-related disasters but recovered quickly to deliver ongoing growth in property values.

The resilience of housing markets after being hammered by severe weather is remarkable. Locations with a history of floods have strongly rising property values. Sometimes there is a short-term hit to local prices, but the impact is not long-lasting. The reality of Australia is that many regional centres and capital cities evolved along the banks of major rivers, which have an alarming tendency to burst their banks. Major floods can be devastating on a human level but seldom have lasting impacts on property markets.

Some of the locations on CoreLogic's top 10 cities or towns for increasing dwelling values since COVID (discussed in detail in chapter 10) are places where weather disasters are frequent. The Mary River snakes through Gympie, a little north of the Sunshine Coast in Queensland, and there have been significant floods at various times in its history, including in 1999 and 2022, but that history of freak weather events has not done any lasting damage to Gympie property values. In the five years from 2020 to 2025, Gympie ranked fourth in the nation for capital growth, with dwelling values rising 94%. Eighth on the list, increasing 89%, was Maryborough in Queensland's Fraser Coast region, also on the Mary River, despite also having a history of floods that includes two devastating events in quick succession at the beginning of 2022. Bundaberg was sixth on the list despite also having a history of floods, being built alongside the Burnett River and experiencing major events in 2010 and 2013.

Townsville has been a stellar performer on property price growth in recent years despite damaging weather in 2019 and 2024 – and at other times, given its location in tropical Far North Queensland. Insurance premiums are scarily high in Townsville thanks to its weather history, but home buyers and investors are evidently undaunted. Suburbs considered to be the most at risk of flooding have exceptional annual growth rates for their property values, including Hermit Park (15% per year over five years) and Rosslea (18%).

Perhaps the most flood-impacted community in Australia is the town of Lismore on the banks of the Wilsons River in New South Wales. Devastating weather events occurred in 2017 and 2022. Property values took a hit following the 2022 event but recovered noticeably in 2024 and 2025.

There is some evidence that property values can rise in weather-impacted locations because of the damage rather than despite it. A major flood can destroy large numbers of houses, rendering them uninhabitable and significantly reducing the supply of homes in the area, thus creating a shortage.

Affordability rules – the best growth often occurs in the cheapest areas

Real estate abounds with myths and misconceptions, particularly about where you get the best price growth. Some of the oldest, and most inaccurate, beliefs about prices refuse to die. Here are some of the most cherished furphies about the best places to own real estate:

- The capital cities outperform the regions.
- The biggest cities show the best growth.
- Suburbs close to the CBD excel on growth.
- The prime upmarket suburbs show the best price uplift.
- Houses always grow faster than apartments.

These are all classic pieces of misinformation. The research ridicules all of them. However you look at them, the statistics show that cheap outperforms expensive – that means, in simple terms, the smaller cities, the outer-ring areas of our biggest cities, regional locations and, more recently, attached dwellings. Many may aspire to live in Toorak or Bondi Beach, but that doesn't translate into high demand because most can't afford the multi-million-dollar price tags. The bulk of buyer demand goes to the more affordable areas. Competition for a scarce resource causes prices to rise, and there are more buyers for a house in Frankston (median price $740,000 in May 2025) than a mansion in Toorak (median house price fluctuating between $4.4 million and $6.4 million in 2024 and 2025, the kind of volatility you don't get in mainstream markets).

Peter Koulizos, a former president of PIPA and known as the "Property Professor", conducted research on behalf of PIPA in

2024 to determine where the biggest growth in house prices had occurred in the 20 years from June 2004 to June 2024. The results refuted the notion that the biggest cities were the best and always outdid the regions – small outdid big, and cheap bettered pricey. Of the 14 major market jurisdictions measured, regional Tasmania recorded the biggest growth over two decades, with values rising 233% – in other words, more than tripling. The rest of the top five was Hobart, Adelaide, regional Victoria and Brisbane. Sydney ranked seventh and Melbourne 11th. The 12th-ranked jurisdiction, Canberra, increased 160%, which means even some of the worst performers recorded exceptional increases in housing values. But the expensive places ranked low on the ladder.

That's the long-term view. The medium-term view was the focus of research by CoreLogic published in 2025 that examined price growth across Australia in the five years since COVID struck, which I analyse in detail elsewhere in the book. Small, affordable regional places dominated the rankings, and the best of the capital cities were Perth and Adelaide – two of the smaller, cheaper ones.

Looking at the short-term view, CoreLogic published in May 2025 its top suburbs for annual growth in property values in the various cities. All of the leading suburbs on its lists for Melbourne and Sydney were at least 20km from the CBDs of those cities, including the top 20 performers in Sydney. In Melbourne the top suburb for 12-month growth was Eumemmerring in the far south-east of the metropolitan area, with a median house price below $600,000 despite the year of high growth. Research director Tim Lawless said the pursuit of affordability meant the weight of buyer demand was directed to cheaper areas, and that was driving higher price growth.

How you can manufacture growth

For a long time, most investors did what is known as "passive investing": they bought a dwelling, let it to a tenant and waited for it to grow in value. Very passive, and also perfectly viable. If you choose your locations wisely, that can work out well over time.

Increasingly, though, investors are seeking more. They want properties with a twist. They want properties where they can value-add, accelerating the wealth process by manufacturing growth.

Here are some common ways to do that.

Renovation

Some investors seek homes that are rundown so they can buy them cheaply and add to their value by renovating. Data from 2023 indicates that Australians spend around $1 billion a month on home renovations. A 2025 report suggested a third of Australian households took on a home renovation project in the previous 12 months. Reality TV shows make this look easy and fun, but it's neither. You really need to know what you're doing; you have to understand a lot to succeed. Some overcapitalise and end up losing money. It's unwise to assume the amount spent on a renovation will lift the property's value by a similar amount or more.

Redevelopment

You can buy a house on a block of land that is zoned for a higher use, such as townhouses or a small block of units. This means you have a rentable house in the short term and a development site in the longer term. A 2025 report from the ABS found that in the past year over 20,000 homes were approved for demolition by owners who planned to build something bigger and better.

As with renovation, though, you need to know what you're doing, because development is risky.

Adding a granny flat or second dwelling

Some residential properties allow you to build a granny flat or a second dwelling, provided the land size and zoning is right. Many investors seek these opportunities, so competition for these types of properties in good locations is very strong. Increasingly, this type of activity is being encouraged by state governments and local councils to help address the housing shortage.

Subdividing

Some houses sit on blocks of land large enough to be subdivided. In 2019 I bought a house on land that can be subdivided into three blocks for houses or four for townhouses. The existing house provided an initial rental return of 5.5%, and it increased in value about 10% in the first 12 months. At some point, I will do the subdivision, turning one property into three or four. That's a great way to accelerate the wealth process.

Conclusion

You should now have a much better understanding of why property values rise. Before you try to put that newfound knowledge into practice, though, I leave you with some final thoughts to guide you on your journey towards wealth through property investing.

What I learnt making mistakes

I've read lots of books about people who succeeded. They all had one thing in common: they made mistakes along the way but learnt from them and thrived.

Here's my big real estate lesson after decades of learning: never sell. Accumulate. How did I learn this? By doing the opposite.

The best property investment I ever made was the first one. It was in a suburb of Ipswich City in the south-west of Greater Brisbane. It was meat-and-potatoes real estate, close to a train station and a short drive to two major highways. There were schools and shops in the area. It cost me $25,000 in the early 1980s. Three years later I sold it for $40,000 (it grew 60% in three years) and moved to an inner-ring suburb of Brisbane.

What was my second-best investment? The next one – a property in Balmoral, an inner-ring suburb of Brisbane about

10 minutes from the CBD, then-underrated and destined for gentrification. It was a modest house but perched on a hill with views of the Brisbane River and the Gateway Bridge. I bought it for $50,000 in the mid-1980s. I drove past it a couple of years ago, and someone had demolished my house and built a mansion on the site. The median price for Balmoral in mid-2025 was $1.75 million, the suburb's long-term growth rate was 12% per year and the rental vacancy rate was 0.7%.

You can see my big mistake, I'm sure. I sold those properties to buy bigger and better ones. I should have kept them as the basis for a property portfolio. The two properties that cost me $75,000 in the 1980s would now collectively be worth around $2.5 million.

The costs of selling and buying again are scary high – commissions, legal fees, stamp duty, this fee, that fee. Avoid them. Buy good real estate and keep it. Then buy more.

Be careful what you wish for

Many people want to accumulate real estate assets so they can retire early. Retirement seems to be the grand vision for many Australians. I often think these people must hate their jobs, because I can't relate to retirement. I love research and I love writing, and I want to keep doing it.

One of my role models is David Attenborough, who celebrated his 99th birthday in May 2025 and was still doing what he loves: making brilliant documentaries about the natural world. Another is Warren Buffett, who turned 94 in August 2024 with a net worth estimated at that time at US$151 billion and was still going to the office every day. He loves what he does and doesn't want to quit.

The other thing about the goal of retiring and living a life of leisure on the back of your property portfolio is that it's essentially fantasy. If you own 20 properties all producing income and growing in value, then you have created financial security, but you've also created a job for yourself. Even if you have property managers taking care of each individual property, you have to manage the managers. You'll be getting emails and phone calls every day seeking decisions on repairs and maintenance. You're not retired; you've traded your day job for a new activity.

Still worth doing, but be careful what you wish for.

Is there a perfect location – a "sweet spot"?

A premise of this book is that location is king. Success in real estate relates to buying in good locations. Where you buy is more important than what you buy or when.

When I speak of a good location, I'm not talking about the exact position in a particular street. I mean the broader location – the town, the municipality, the precinct. I mean a cluster of suburbs that benefits from the same advantages.

You might target a coastal enclave of suburbs with commuter train links, a major hospital and a major commercial employment node nearby, where vacancies are low and rents are rising, and there are government plans to create new facilities. Such a location ticks lots of boxes – it has good real estate bones and identifiable drivers of growth .

But what about drilling down to street level? What about the precise position within that cluster of privileged suburbs? You might consider the possibility of what some analysts call "the sweet spot" – the exact, perfect position amid a series of key features.

I believe the three key things to be near to, but not too near to, are public transport, schools and shops. It's good to be close to schools, but you don't want to live across the road from a school, where parents are dropping off and picking up every day. Proximity to public transport is beneficial, but right beside a commuter train station might be a horror story. Being able to walk to shops is fantastic, but directly opposite a regional shopping centre? No, thank you.

The sweet spot, I believe, is 200 metres from each. Of course, it would be almost impossible to find a property that ticks all your other boxes and happens to be located 200 metres from the commuter train station, the local high school and a neighbourhood shopping centre, but it doesn't need to be quite so exact. Near enough is probably good enough.

A side street off a major suburban arterial route and within a few hundred metres of the local school, a train station and a shopping centre is a good place to be. If there's parkland in the vicinity as well, so much the better.

How I do what I do

James Clear described the human brain as a "prediction machine" in the global bestseller *Atomic Habits*:

> Whenever you experience something repeatedly ... your brain begins noticing what is important, sorting through the details and highlighting the relevant cues ... With enough practice, you can pick up on the cues that predict certain outcomes without consciously thinking about it.

This quote encapsulates how I accurately forecast the out-performers in residential real estate. I don't have a secret recipe or algorithm. I don't feed data into a computer and ask it to spit out "the best place to buy". My process is not all about statistics. I do have a process, and I do absorb information about prices and rents and a host of other factors. However, in essence, I make a judgment call. My brain has a conversation with my gut.

I've been observing markets for over 40 years. Name a regional centre or LGA anywhere in Australia and I can speak for 15 minutes about the location, its economy and its property market. I have a fundamental understanding of all the towns and suburban precincts that matter in Australia. That's all in my head.

Every day I'm talking to people – builders, buyers' agents, researchers, valuers, businesspeople, property managers, investors – and sometimes a scrap of information contained in a comment is important. It gels with something I've seen in the sales activity numbers or the rental data. An article in my daily newsfeed might announce the start of ground works on an infrastructure project, and there will be a Eureka moment. A lifetime of experience has given me the instincts that matter.

I spent a weekend in Kingaroy in 2022 and came away knowing it would outperform. So much was happening that people outside the region didn't know about. It eventually ranked number two in Australia on growth in property values in that 2025 CoreLogic report.

I visited Bundaberg because my in-laws lived there, and I could feel the prosperity underlying its property market. I knew it had a strong economy and a great lifestyle. When they announced plans for a $1 billion hospital, I knew it was time to talk about this location as a future outperformer. It ranked number six in Australia for capital growth in the five years to 2025.

For many years I saw Adelaide as the nation's most underrated city, with beaches, a fabulous hills district and three major wine regions. It had wonderful streetscapes and affordable prices. Eventually, I thought, Australia would realise its potential. When CommSec's *State of the States* report started raising South Australia's ranking (and eventually it hit the number one spot),

I knew it was time to shout about the city's real estate prospects. At the time of writing, the Adelaide market has been rising for five years and shows no sign of slowing down. In *The Global Liveability Index 2025* published by the Economist Intelligence Unit in June, Adelaide made the worldwide top 10. CoreLogic's *Pain and Gain* report, also published in June 2025, found that 95% of property sales nationwide in the March 2025 quarter made a profit for the vendor, with Adelaide achieving the highest nominal gain in the nation at $385,000 and 99% of Adelaide vendors recording a profit.

I'm aware that some businesses have been devoting considerable resources to creating an algorithm that predicts future hotspots. Lazy practitioners who call themselves "buyers' agents" are asking ChatGPT to tell them the best place in Australia to buy. I fear for the investors who rely on "advice" from such people. At the risk of appearing a dinosaur in the digital age, I doubt the people trying to make AI do the work for them will ever succeed; real estate has too many subtle and intangible elements. Asking a bot to scour the metaverse and provide the next hotspot is inviting a presentation on the great seething mass of misinformation that pervades real estate coverage. Human judgment based on knowledge and research will always play a key role.

About the author

Terry Ryder has been a specialist researcher and writer on Australian residential property for more than four decades. His career began when he was appointed Property Editor of *The Courier Mail* in 1982 and continued when he worked as the Property Correspondent and Acting Property Editor at the *Australian Financial Review*.

For more than 20 years, Terry operated his own real estate research and publicity business, providing research and writing services to investors, property developers, agencies, valuers and other professional firms providing services to the real estate industry.

In 2006, Terry created the website hotspotting.com.au, which provides reports and subscription services to property investors advising the best places to buy. This was expanded in mid-2024 with the launch of the Hotspotting Research Hub, which provides real-time data and analytics for every property market in Australia.

This and other innovations culminated in Hotspotting being named AI Innovator of the Year in the Property Industry in the Momentum Media Australian AI Awards in 2024.

Hotspotting's core mission is to identify the future out-performers in residential real estate throughout Australia. It also provides a range of services to real estate professionals and businesses including custom reports, strategy and mentoring. Terry has remained active within the real estate media landscape. He is a monthly columnist for the *Australian Property Investor* magazine, has been a regular contributor to *Money* magazine for 15 years and is a columnist for Australia's largest comparison website, Canstar.

Terry is frequently interviewed by radio stations and television current affairs programs on real estate issues. He has appeared on *A Current Affair*, *Sunrise*, *4 Corners*, *Your Money Your Call* and *Money Talks* with Peter Switzer. He is also regularly quoted in real estate magazines including *Australian Property Investor*, *Smart Property Investor* and *Your Investment Property*, and business magazines including *Money* as well as Australia's major metropolitan newspapers. He is a regular speaker at seminars and conferences across Australia and overseas with his broadcasts and podcasts via social media followed by tens of thousands of Australians. Terry is also the co-host of the Ticker TV program, *The Property Playbook*, which provides insights and strategies for property investment.

Why Property Values Rise is Terry's fifth book.

Contact Terry Ryder

T: 07 5494 2575
M: 0408 011 595
E: ryder@hotspotting.com.au

**Ryder
Property
Research**

Hotspotting
by Ryder

Be better with business books

MAJOR STREET

We hope you enjoy reading this book. We'd love you to post a review on social media or your favourite bookseller site. Please include the hashtag #majorstreetpublishing.

Major Street Publishing specialises in business, leadership, personal finance and motivational non-fiction books. If you'd like to receive regular updates about new Major Street books, email info@majorstreet.com.au and ask to be added to our mailing list.

Visit majorstreet.com.au to find out more about our books (print, audio and ebooks), and read news and reviews.

We'd love you to follow us on social media.

- in linkedin.com/company/major-street-publishing
- f facebook.com/MajorStreetPublishing
- ⌾ instagram.com/majorstreetpublishing
- ✖ @MajorStreetPub